The more focused you are, the easier everything becomes. Bethanne has put together a practical and proven set of steps that will help you focus on what matters. What you do every day will do more for you than what you do once in a while. Spend a few minutes with Bethanne every morning and set yourself up to succeed!

Mark LeBlanc
Author of *Growing Your Business*
and *Never Be the Same*

About Bethanne Kronick:

Bethanne has been a teacher all her life. She's passionate about helping busy people find a more balanced, successful life. Through classes and workshops for organizations and businesses, she helps people live with less stress and find more time and energy for the things they are passionate about.

Bethanne is a proud member of the National Speakers Association (NSA) and the National Association of Professional Organizers (NAPO). In May of 2007, Bethanne became one of the first Professional Organizers in the nation to receive the Certified Professional Organizer designation (CPO).

When she's not working with clients, Bethanne can be found in her rowing shell training for the next race! Being outdoors and in her boat provides her with the motivation and energy to help people. Her other passions include her family, friends and eating ice cream!

SIMPLIFY!
One Day at a Time

365 Ways to Improve Productivity

Bethanne Kronick

SIMPLIFY! One Day at a Time — 365 Ways to
Improve Productivity

ISBN – 10: 0-6159-1117-X
ISBN – 13: 978-0-6159-1117-5 (SIMPLIFY!)

DEDICATION

For my dad...my "Poopa"--
the one with whom I could sit next to
on a rock by a lake
and have an amazing conversation,
without saying a word...

You would be so proud...

You continue to inspire me...

I miss you.

FOREWORD

The true measure of any person is not what they say, but what they do —especially over time. How they respond to real-life challenges, business or personal, and how they help others gain more of what *they* really want. People who truly LOVE helping others to get more of what they want are rare in this world. Bethanne is in this league.

Having known Bethanne for 25-plus years, I have seen the power of her empathctic character, skill-sets, intuition, problem-solving abilities, and passion for helping others, become a successful company called SIMPLIFY! She has the ability to turn the attitudes and work habits of a sluggish, unmotivated group of individuals into a cohesively operating team, excited to take on the challenges they face. This is a skill *and* an art––and she is a seasoned pro!

She has also been able to imbed into her clients' mind-sets, her own mantra of "Life-Work Balance," which is of *massive* value for the small, mid-sized, and larger companies she works with. She lives this mantra, and coaches it to her clients. Her commitment to helping individuals and organizations alike attain a higher, more organized level of professionalism is impressive. And most importantly, her character, trust-worthiness, skill-sets, attentiveness to those she is working with, and her work ethic, are rock-solid!

This book of her guidance should help start your day off on a positive note, giving you both direction and insight to Simplify One Day at a Time, while getting more done, more effectively, with less stress. SIMPLIFY!

Michael A. Boylan
Best-selling author of **The Power To Get In**, **TEETH**, and **Accelerants**
Founder, The Reach For Me Network

INTRODUCTION

I have been working with people in all capacities of organizations and companies of all sizes since 2002. I find most people are overwhelmed, overloaded and overstressed. It brings me great joy to provide them with tools, strategies and ideas and watch the positive outcome that results as people regain control of their lives.

It is these experiences of watching people improve the quality of their lives that inspired me to write this book. My hope is that you will set aside a few moments every morning before your day launches into high gear, maybe with a cup of tea or coffee and read the day's idea, tip or reminder. SIMPLIFY! your life one day at a time!

Enjoy!

Simply,

Bethanne

bethanne@simplifynw.com

SIMPLIFY! TERMS AND CONCEPTS YOU'LL SEE THROUGHOUT THE BOOK:

Focus Time – In today's overly busy and information-saturated world, it can be difficult to find adequate time to get your work done. Set aside designated blocks of time called "Focus Time" to work on projects that require higher levels of focus and attention. Block segments of 30-90 minutes at a time and make an effort to limit interruptions, distractions and conscientiously avoid the temptation to multitask. The results from this practice are higher quality work and faster progress with less stress. Use a desktop timer to help track your time. To maximize your commitment to using Focus Time, we encourage blocking it as an appointment on your calendar so it doesn't get bumped by other lower value tasks.

Action System – There are many options (paper or digital) to track active projects and tasks. Choose a paper calendar, your email program calendar, a task list (paper or electronic), an action folder located in your email folders, a tickler file or a combination of several. Having a system will help ensure you keep on top of individual and recurring projects.

5 Decisions – A strategy to process incoming information: email, incoming digital and paper documents, voicemail, requests of yourself or from others. Make one of five decisions to process each item: **toss or delete**, **delegate or forward**, **do it now or reply**, **file for reference** or **place in your Action System**.

Capture Cards – Keep on track in meetings and during focused work times by using some form of capture media for "dumping" thoughts and ideas from your brain that aren't necessary for the immediate work but are things you want to be sure to remember. Use notecards, a small pad, a tape recorder or an electronic device to record thoughts, ideas and to-dos to revisit later and enter in your Action System.

JANUARY 1

Happy New Year!
Set goals, not resolutions.

▧ ▧ ▧

What better time to set a goal of getting the year off to an organized start! Look around you, both at home and at work, and ask yourself, "What systems and spaces need an overhaul?" Getting organized is one of the top New Year's resolutions. Instead of having a "resolution" set a goal of improving your organization and productivity. This book will give you tips to help!

JANUARY 2

Write down your three
"must do's" for the day.

■　■　■

Determine what the three most critical things
are for you to get done today. Write them on a
post-it to attach to your computer, or on a pad
that will travel with you. Dive into these tasks as
soon as possible and make them your focus. As
much of your time and energy as possible should
be dedicated to accomplishing them. Don't stray!

JANUARY 3

Appreciate every moment
of your day today.

▨   ▨   ▨

Time is precious. Being in the moment with everything you do and everyone you do it with is something you can teach yourself to do. Take a deep breath when you tend to get distracted. Make a conscious effort to be present with the things you do and the people you are with instead of just coasting through your day.

JANUARY 4

*Develop a cue or reminder for a
new habit you are developing.*

▩ ▩ ▩

Set a timer, use a post-it note in a helpful
location, schedule an electronic reminder, wear
your watch on the opposite wrist... whatever it
takes to remind you to help get that new habit to
become routine!

JANUARY 5

※　※　※

The past is behind – we must learn from it. The future is ahead – we must prepare for it. The present is now – we must live in it.

- Thomas S. Monson

JANUARY 6

*Be aware of the people
who distract you today.*

■　■　■

Do co-workers show up in your cubicle or office
on a regular basis for questions or conversations? Ask colleagues to allow you a minute or
two to finish what you are doing so you can give
them your full attention. If their issue isn't
urgent and you have other higher priority items
to take care of, don't be afraid to ask if they can
come back later, email you the question or, if
appropriate, ask them to schedule an
appointment to meet at a later time.

JANUARY 7

Review your routines.

▨　▨　▨

Do you have any routines that need improvement? Think of one that you could tweak today. Routines need to be adjusted as life changes. Be creative but practical as you make shifts. Be sure to give yourself time to let the new routine become habit.

JANUARY 8

Challenge yourself to focus on doing one thing at a time today!

▦   ▦   ▦

When you try to do multiple things (that require brainpower) at the same time, it doesn't serve you well. It takes longer, you're not as efficient and it's stressful. Multitasking is a myth!

JANUARY 9

*Check your energy level
throughout the day.*

▦   ▦   ▦

Developing the habit of monitoring your energy
level is important to be able to pace yourself.
Make an effort to operate more like a marathon
runner (controlled and consistent) than a
sprinter (cruising from crisis to crisis).

JANUARY 10

Clearly define projects.

■   ■   ■

When you take on a new project, whether at work or at home, be sure you have clarity about its scope and expectations. To complete your project successfully, here are some considerations: know what you are trying to achieve, what's involved and any time constraints or deadlines. Take time to ensure you have the information you need to finish it well.

JANUARY 11

Go on an information diet!

◼ ◼ ◼

You are surrounded by an endless amount of information in this digital age — much more than you can digest in a 24-hour day. It can be stressful seeing all the stuff you "should" be reading. Determine the magazines, catalogs and e-newsletters which are most important to you. Stop your subscriptions or unsubscribe to the rest.

JANUARY 12

Lesson Learned:

■   ■   ■

What a huge relief it was for an employee who grew tired of seeing stacks of decades-old journals, magazines and documents when she gave herself permission to let them go. She now has a cleaner, more efficient office — free of clutter! She feels lighter, more free and happier!

JANUARY 13

*Take time to learn something
today that will help you
work more efficiently.*

※　　※　　※

Increasing your profound knowledge will help
you get more done in less time. Attend a webinar
or spend time with a mentor. By learning to be
the best at what you do, you will do it better
and faster.

JANUARY 14

Send handwritten thank you notes.

■   ■   ■

If you have a positive meeting with a prospect, client, customer or colleague today, send them a handwritten note thanking them. Handwritten notes and cards are such a rarity anymore you will stand out from the crowd and you might just make someone's day!

JANUARY 15

Process action items from meetings before starting other tasks.

■   ■   ■

When you return from a meeting, be sure to put any to-do's on your calendar, task list or in your tickler file. Do this before you move on to the next thing! It's the pits going back to a follow-up meeting not having accomplished the action items you were tasked with only because they were written in a folder that was filed away after your meeting.

JANUARY 16

Printed information—before
you file it, ask yourself,
"Do I really need it?"

■   ■   ■

Only 20% of the paper that people save ever gets referred to again. Be honest with yourself about how important it is to save paper documents. So much information can be accessed electronically today, allowing people to save less. Remember, you'll need to purge regularly. It's much easier and quicker when only the important things are saved.

JANUARY 17

Schedule time to streamline your organization systems.

▓ ▓ ▓

Systems need maintenance on a regular basis. Develop a routine to tidy up your desk. You'll be much happier to work in your office when it's organized. Many people find Fridays are a great day to get things back in order so that the following week starts off on the right foot.

JANUARY 18

Create a "someday maybe" list.

■   ■   ■

Designate a place (journal, paper file or electronic list) where you keep track of your "someday maybe" ideas. Whether it's a book you want to read, a computer program you want to learn, a place you want to visit, write it down so you don't have to clog your memory with unnecessary information.

JANUARY 19

■ ■ ■

Sometimes the best thing to do with your time is to do NOTHING!

—Kelsey Johansen (my wise niece at age 12)

JANUARY 20

*Limit distractions
during your work day.*

▨　▨　▨

If possible, turn your cell phone off when you are
at your desk. If it's necessary to keep it on, put it
on silent or place it in a drawer and check it
occasionally. If you are on call and need to be
accessible, put your phone on vibrate and
answer only the calls that are necessary. Cell
phones can be huge productivity killers. Do what
you can to minimize the distraction.

JANUARY 21

Everything you are faced with today is a choice. Take control and make smart ones!

■   ■   ■

Whether it's the clothes you selected this morning, what you ate for breakfast, if you'll go to the gym after work, or how well prepared you are for this afternoon's meeting, life is one choice after another. Take control and make choices that will result in you being productive, successful, healthy and happy.

JANUARY 22

Tackle high value tasks first.

■ ■ ■

Develop the habit of diving into your most important task first thing each morning before you do anything else. It takes discipline to tackle your major task first. Work through it with as few interruptions as possible and enjoy the reward of getting it done promptly!

JANUARY 23

Be cautious about saying YES to requests of your time.

※　　※　　※

Think carefully about the requests others place on your time. Consider how the requests will impact your own high priority tasks before you say yes. Don't take on someone else's requests at the expense of your own top priority tasks. If you need to decline, say no logically, firmly and tactfully.

JANUARY 24

Select the right communication tool.

■　　■　　■

If you know someone's preferred communication style, do your best to connect with them that way. Some people prefer having live conversations whether they are on the phone or face-to-face. Others prefer electronic communication. Making sure they receive your message or request in their preferred mode will help keep projects moving forward.

JANUARY 25

Declutter an area in your office that is driving you crazy!

▨   ▨   ▨

For every item, ask yourself — do you use it, need it or love it? If not, get rid of it. Too much stuff in your immediate surroundings can be stressful and keep you from being productive. Going through an area (even a drawer), sorting through things, purging and reorganizing will energize you. Toss things that are old or broken. Give away things that others could make use of. It feels SO good!

JANUARY 26

Lesson Learned:

■   ■   ■

A manager made a huge dent in eliminating
email in his inbox by learning how to set rules
in his email program to move messages that he
didn't need to be concerned about directly to
folders. What a huge time saver!

JANUARY 27

Update your calendar regularly
— at work and at home.

▓   ▓   ▓

Get in the habit of immediately putting meetings and appointments on your calendar. This will alleviate any embarrassing moments when you don't show up. It also decreases the chances of getting double booked.

JANUARY 28

Have some fun at work today!
Laugh and have a good time!

■ ■ ■

Work is a large part of your life — it should be joyful. If you are happy, you will be more likely to excel at your work.

JANUARY 29

*Reduce desktop clutter
on your screen.*

▨   ▨   ▨

If your computer desktop is a mess, take time today to clean it up. Your desktop is a place for documents, files and program shortcuts that you *actively* use. Delete or file items that you no longer access on a frequent basis. It will be much more visually appealing and your computer will be happier and run more efficiently as well!

JANUARY 30

Identify something that you have been procrastinating on getting done. Attack it today!

■　■　■

To make progress, break it down into smaller tasks. Write these tasks down. Take on the first one and get going! You'll wonder what took you so long...

JANUARY 31

*Streamline the system you use
for tracking your to-do's.*

▩   ▩   ▩

Everyone uses a different system depending on
their style and needs. Some use a paper calendar,
others use a paper to-do list, some use an electronic task list. Determine what fits you best and
keep everything in that one place. It alleviates
duplication of efforts, post-it notes everywhere,
or forgetting things because you have no system.

FEBRUARY 1

*Recognize and respond to
signs of overload.*

■　　■　　■

It's easy to get overloaded. Do your best to
recognize when it is beginning to happen so you
can respond effectively. If you get that overwhelmed feeling during the day today, here are
some ways you can respond: slow down and
breathe, clarify your priorities, simplify your
tasks by breaking them down into smaller ones,
discard what's truly not important, re-energize
and go!

FEBRUARY 2

※　※　※

Every day, say this mantra out loud:
"I choose to be happy today. I will
be faced with challenges, but I will
choose to stay positive and happy.
Happiness is mandatory in my life."
– Kellie Poulsen-Grill

FEBRUARY 3

Tackle time-wasting habits.

■ ■ ■

It's easy to waste time on tasks that are low priority. Write on a card or post-it note two things you have control of that waste time, and make an effort to minimize the time you spend on them today. Once you determine what they are, you'll be much more sensitive to using your time for high priority and meaningful activities.

FEBRUARY 4

Separate action items from your notes at meetings.

▨ ▨ ▨

When you attend a meeting, have one location where you take general notes and a separate place for writing down action items. Following up on action items is critical. When they get mixed in with your notes, they are much more difficult to find and you might miss an important task needing follow through.

FEBRUARY 5

Schedule time on your calendar to prepare in advance for trips.

■ ■ ■

If you travel for your work either occasionally or regularly, planning ahead is critical. Last minute planning increases the possibility of not having the materials, information, supplies or products you need resulting in a less than stellar performance and poor results.

FEBRUARY 6

What are the things that zap your energy during the day?

◼ ◼ ◼

Be aware of these activities (and sometimes even people) so you can do your best to steer clear of them. Work to balance your life so there are more activities that energize you than those that tend to drain you.

FEBRUARY 7

*Seek out projects that are
congruent with your passions.*

■ ■ ■

If you don't have any projects, clients, customers
or activities in your routine at work you are
passionate about, spend some time today finding one that you can add to your workload. It's
important to have something or someone in your
line-up during your day that motivates you,
energizes you and gets you excited. It's a win-
win for all.

FEBRUARY 8

Improve your ability to focus by limiting distractions.

■　　■　　■

The average person faces outside or self-imposed interruptions on average every three minutes. There are so many distractors these days: email, Facebook, cell phones, our own thoughts, people dropping by the office… Be aware of how these distractors impact your productivity and develop the habit and discipline to focus on the task, project or person at hand.

FEBRUARY 9

Lesson Learned:

■   ■   ■

One company issued headphones with the company logo imprinted on them to new employees. The headphones did double duty helping minimize noise in the cubical environment as well as serving as a visual cue to other co-workers when they needed to stay focused on a task and not be disrupted.

FEBRUARY 10

"Time block" for tasks that require time and attention.

███   ███   ███

Schedule appointments with yourself (and YES, actually enter them on your calendar) for the tasks that need to get done in your day so you have the time you need to accomplish them.

FEBRUARY 11

*Create a "drop spot"
at home and at work.*

■ ■ ■

Have a location in your office (and at home)
where you always put things you use on a regular basis (keys, sunglasses, briefcase, purse, etc.)
and train yourself to use it. By determining a
specific location for these things, it takes the
guesswork out of where to find them. If there are
other people involved, be sure to instruct them
as to how and where to put things so everyone
can find them.

FEBRUARY 12

*Process your mail in the
same spot every day.*

▨   ▨   ▨

Take a couple of minutes to do a quick sort.
Have a recycle bin nearby so the junk mail can be
tossed in it immediately and only keep what's
important. Sort what remains into items to read,
to be filed, delegated or needing action. Using a
process will alleviate handling the mail several
times.

FEBRUARY 13

*Are you using your strengths
in doing your job?*

■　■　■

Teams are made up of people with varying
strengths and weaknesses. Do your best to be
operating in your strengths so you will perform
at your best. Redefining responsibilities can be
considered to maximize the strengths and
talents of a team.

FEBRUARY 14

*Refer to attachments in
the body of your email.*

▨　　▨　　▨

If you send an email with attachments, mention the attachments in the body of your email. Sometimes attachments can be overlooked if there is no mention of them. Always check to make sure you've included the attachments before pressing "send."

FEBRUARY 15

Take control of your stuff.

■　　■　　■

It's easy to get overwhelmed and let your stuff
control you. Whether it's your inbox, your paper
documents, or your calendar events, be sure
you control them today and not the other way
around. Let your systems kick in and your
commitment to being productive rule!

*Life is a great and wondrous
mystery, and the only thing we
know that we have for sure
is right here, right now.
Don't miss it.*

– *Leo Buscaglia*

FEBRUARY 17

*When you are not actively
working on email,
minimize your email screen.*

■　■　■

The inbox can be addictive. It's easier to focus on
your work when you are not being tempted to
regularly glance at your inbox. If it's minimized,
it takes away the temptation.

FEBRUARY 18

*Keep a box next to your garbage
can for paper recycling.*

▓   ▓   ▓

Reuse the back side of single-sided printing for
scratch paper. Do what you can to practice
sustainable and "green" habits at work and at
home, too!

FEBRUARY 19

*Unplug when you spend time
with people today.*

■   ■   ■

When you spend time with your family, friends
or colleagues today, set the example and turn off
your cell phone. Enjoy high quality time together
without the distraction of the beeps and vibra-
tions of phones, texts and emails. You can pick
up messages later. Your undivided attention will
improve your professional and personal
relationships.

FEBRUARY 20

*Don't let interruptions
sabotage your day.*

■   ■   ■

Take control and create an environment to be as
interruption-free as possible while working on
your projects and to-do's. Close your door, turn
off your cell phone, and let your landline go to
voicemail. Set an appointment with yourself on
your calendar so your time can't be booked
otherwise. Productivity will abound!

FEBRUARY 21

*Review your calendar before
checking email each day.*

■　■　■

Make an effort to look at your calendar and your
plan for the day first, before you dive into your
inbox. Email can be addictive. Checking it first
thing in the morning can often derail accomplishing the tasks that are highest priority. Work
on these first and then check email.

FEBRUARY 22

*Plan to use vacation time
on a regular basis,
even it means a "stay-cation."*

▧　　▧　　▧

Americans spend a lot of time working. 34% of Americans typically don't use all their vacation days! Vacations and stay-cations are not only fun, but beneficial to your productivity. Is it time to put one on the calendar?

FEBRUARY 23

Lesson Learned:

▓   ▓   ▓

An employee did some much needed re-prioritizing at work and is now thrilled to have more time to spend with her son doing the activities they love to do together: camping, hiking and traveling!

FEBRUARY 24

Carry "work to go" when attending meetings or appointments.

▧　　▧　　▧

If you are early, or someone is late for an appointment, make the most of your time by having reading materials with you or a small project you can work on. (Or sometimes, enjoying a bit of unexpected free time can be nice to just relax and do nothing!)

FEBRUARY 25

*Track notes from meetings
and phone calls in your
email contact manager.*

■   ■   ■

Write notes from phone calls or topics discussed
in meetings in a person's individual profile in
your contact manager. Having these notes will
help remind you of details that may be difficult
to remember, especially if you don't have contact
with the person for a while.

FEBRUARY 26

Location matters when it comes to having quick access to things that you need.

▦　▦　▦

Be sure you have convenient, easy access to the tools and equipment you need to do your job effectively. If things like a label maker, outbox, scanner/printer, etc., are used frequently, be sure you have them easily accessible in your work space.

Discover your passions.

■   ■   ■

Do you know what you are passionate about, at work or outside of work? If not, take some time to figure it out. Sometimes it's easy to get caught up in the "should-a's" and lose touch with what you are passionate about. Consider your talents, skills, knowledge, experience and the things that bring you joy and make you want to jump out of bed in the morning.

FEBRUARY 28

Review the system you use for storing your electronic documents.

■   ■   ■

It may have been a while since you have looked at the system you use for storing documents electronically, or maybe you never really set one up. Putting thought into creating and maintaining a system that makes sense will save you time when you need to file or retrieve a document.

MARCH 1

Bookmark your breaks.

■   ■   ■

If you have to take a break from working on a project or a task, make a note where you left off. If and when you need to attend a meeting or shift your attention to another task or person, take a brief moment to write a note as to where you are leaving off on your current project. It will alleviate wasting time trying to figure out where to begin when you return.

MARCH 2

※　※　※

The Future is something which everyone reaches at the rate of sixty minutes an hour, whatever he does, whoever he is. – C.S. Lewis

MARCH 3

Find an accountability partner.

■ ■ ■

What new habit are you trying to implement in your life? New routines can be difficult to establish. You will be three times more successful if you ask someone to partner with you. Develop key questions you can ask each other to keep you on track with new routines and encourage each other through the successes and the challenges. It's not only worth it, but it's a lot more fun!

MARCH 4

Identify a skill that you need to improve upon and research how you can do it.

▩ ▩ ▩

Maybe you don't type fast enough, or read fast enough. Maybe your file system needs help. You will save yourself time and energy by finding solutions to these and other issues.

MARCH 5

Schedule a date with yourself to do a quarterly review of your goals.

▨ ▨ ▨

Check your progress and update your goals accordingly. To achieve success, goals need to be assessed and re-assessed. And what a great opportunity to see the progress you've made!

MARCH 6

Get plenty of sunshine and/or vitamin D to energize your body, mind and soul.

▪   ▪   ▪

If because of your locale, you need to purchase a full spectrum light, it's highly recommended. Talk with your doctor if you think you may need a vitamin D supplement. The energy you get from sunshine improves your mood, makes you more fun to be around and helps you get more done!

MARCH 7

*Create a space for items
you need on the go.*

■   ■   ■

Establish a location and container (basket, bin, bag, etc.) in your office where you put things that need to travel with you (to your home, for errands, to school, etc.). By designating a specific location, the things you need will be in one place and ready to go when you are, instead of having to take time to locate them.

MARCH 8

Create a system for capturing people-related reminders.

▦   ▦   ▦

Create file folders or a digital list for people you interact with on a regular basis. Put notes and reminders here of items you want to share or discuss with them at your next meeting. Having an organized location for reminders eliminates two potential problems: forgetting these ideas because you didn't write them down, and becoming an interruption in your co-worker's work flow when you hit them with multiple calls or emails.

MARCH 9

Lesson Learned:

■   ■   ■

Recently a six year old boy went on a hike. He noticed an unusual log and, using his imagination, decided it was shaped like a "cool" dinosaur. At one point, he remarked about the adults who had rushed ahead, "They are in such a rush they missed the good stuff!" Take time today to experience the good stuff!

MARCH 10

*Use "NRN"—"No Reply Necessary,"
as you close an email if you don't
need a response.*

❖ ❖ ❖

Share this acronym with co-workers. Giving
people the permission to not hit "reply" can be
a time saver for both you and your recipient. It
takes the guess work out of it for them.

MARCH 11

*Be realistic about how you plan
and use your time today.*

■　■　■

The law of forced efficiency is a reminder that
there is never enough time to do everything,
but there is always enough time to do the most
important thing.

MARCH 12

Use the "rip and read" technique with magazines.

▨   ▨   ▨

Simply tear out the pages you wish to keep and put them in a file to read later. Recycle the remainder of the magazines so they are not cluttering your workspace. Assuming you are not at the library or in a bookstore, this is a great strategy for paring down your reading material.

MARCH 13

Do you need to put yourself on a social media diet?

■　　■　　■

Set clear boundaries and limits on how much time you spend on these sites each day. Social media is a wonderful thing, but can be addicting and keep you from doing your high priority tasks and the things you are passionate about.

MARCH 14

Review the system you use to store your reference files. Is it working for you or does it need to be revamped?

▓   ▓   ▓

File systems need to be revisited and updated on a regular basis. Ask yourself these questions: Are your categories still current? Can you find what you need? Do your files need purging? Are there files that need to be archived?

MARCH 15

*Be proactive and accomplish
a task in only the time it takes
and move on.*

■　■　■

It's easy to extend the amount of time a task
takes if it's available, even if it's not necessary.
Use the extra time to get something else done.

*Success is what happens **to** you; significance is what happens **through** you.* – Peter Hirsch

MARCH 17

Everything you do today should be related to the goals and three "must do's" that you've determined for the day.

■ ■ ■

Whether it is email you are sending, phone calls you are making, meetings you are holding, etc., keep your goals in sight.

MARCH 18

Be realistic about the time it takes to accomplish the tasks in your day.

▨   ▨   ▨

When you are planning your schedule, be conscious of the time it takes to complete certain tasks. Don't cut yourself short so that you end up not having time for the things you've planned. Consider giving yourself 15 minutes of extra cushion time.

MARCH 19

Remind yourself of your vision and goals for the day. This awareness will be energizing!

■   ■   ■

Reviewing your goals is not only important for planning purposes, but it's also important to be able to have the energy you need to accomplish what's on your plate.

MARCH 20

Get the best help when you need it.

◼   ◼   ◼

If there is something you need assistance with
or something you can delegate, ask for help.
Remember though, it's your responsibility to
follow up with whoever is helping you. Make a
note in your action system or on your calendar
to check in with the person to get a progress
check. If they beat you to following up, hooray!

MARCH 21

If you have more than one computer monitor, use them efficiently.

■   ■   ■

Using multiple monitors is known to significantly increase people's productivity IF they are used effectively. That doesn't mean having one monitor watching the football game or the latest sale on Nordstrom.com. Use your monitors to have information that you need to view simultaneously. If you don't need them all, minimize all windows and let your screensaver keep you from getting distracted. That means even minimizing your inbox if you don't need it.

MARCH 22

Take 10 minutes to read an article or blog today that will improve your knowledge.

▨　▨　▨

You are surrounded by information that can help you be better at what you do. Invest a small amount of time every day to take advantage of it. It's a nice way to take a break, too!

MARCH 23

Lesson Learned:

▦ ▦ ▦

A manager found that she could get an immense amount of work done if she scheduled herself to work off-site two afternoons per month. If for some reason it wasn't convenient to go to a satellite office, she'd work in a small conference room in the building. Working away from her desk on a regular basis substantially reduced the amount of interruptions in her day.

MARCH 24

Think before you click "send."

■　■　■

Before you compose an email, ask yourself first if it's necessary, and second, if it's the best mode of communication. Sometimes an email isn't necessary at all. Those short one or two word responses can often be frustrating for the recipient and a poor use of time for both people. Other times, it may be more effective to pick up the phone and have a conversation.

MARCH 25

What can you delegate that you've been procrastinating about?

■　■　■

Identify a task or project you have been procrastinating about that would make sense to delegate to someone else. If there is someone who has a better skill set than you have and can accomplish the task more easily, or if they have time to get it done in a more timely manner, it makes most sense to pass it on so it gets done.

MARCH 26

Schedule your day considering your energy highs and lows.

■　■　■

When are you most energetic during the day? And least energetic? Schedule your day accordingly. Activities and tasks requiring high energy should be scheduled during the time of day when you have the most pizzazz. Schedule the tasks that tend to be "no brainers" during your low times.

MARCH 27

Don't plan to work overtime.

▨　▨　▨

If you anticipate staying late, you will be less efficient with your time. Parkinson's Law explains that activities tend to expand to fill the time available for them. Keep your work day at 8 hours and you'll work harder to get your high priority tasks done in that timeframe.

MARCH 28

*Don't take your cell phone
to meetings.*

▨   ▨   ▨

Eliminate the temptation to be disrupted at
meetings by just leaving your phone in your
office or car. The disturbance isn't fair to you or
the others attending the event. If you are on call
and need to be accessible, put your phone on
vibrate and put it somewhere (in a bag or briefcase) where others won't hear the vibration.

Create checklists for routine tasks.

▨   ▨   ▨

Think about the activities and processes you do
routinely and create checklists for them. Using
checklists brings clarity and saves time by not
having to reinvent the wheel every time you
repeat a task.

░ ░ ░

It's not enough to be busy; so are the ants. The question is, what are we busy about? — Henry David Thoreau

MARCH 31

Create individual project file folders for each project you are working on.

■　■　■

Put them in a location where they are easy to access. You may have project files in hard copy and/or electronic form. Convenience is important when it comes to items you use frequently.

APRIL 1

*Delay your answer when you are
asked to take on something new.*

▦　　▦　　▦

When someone asks you to take on something
that you are uncertain about, don't react and
immediately say YES. Instead, reply with "I'll get
back to you." It's easy to want to be the good guy
and always say YES to things you're asked to do.
There are only so many hours in the day and it's
important to constantly and realistically check in
with your priorities before committing to more.

APRIL 2

Laugh! Have fun!
At and away from work!

■   ■   ■

The benefits of fun and laughter to our bodies, hearts, minds and souls are immense. Instead of taking time to identify those benefits now, go begin your day with some fun!

APRIL 3

Create a "Master List" for clarity.

※　※　※

If you are overwhelmed with a lot of different projects on your plate, it may be helpful to create a Master List. Prioritize your list and move items from the Master List to your daily action file or to-do list as time allows. Keep your Master List in either print or electronic form to give you an overview of all the tasks and projects requiring your time and energy.

APRIL 4

*Designate a location for bills
and important information
at the office and at home .*

■ ■ ■

Having a specific spot will prevent these
documents from getting misplaced. Ultimately
once mail is sorted, bills and important information should be delivered to this location right
away so that it's done.

APRIL 5

*Limit your time with
energy "vampires."*

■   ■   ■

If you notice a person or people in your life who
are negative and suck you dry of your energy,
find a polite way to spend less time with them if
possible. Make positive choices about whom you
spend your time with. Life is much more fun
when you spend it with people who make you
feel good!

APRIL 6

Lesson Learned:

■   ■   ■

A successful small business owner finally got tired of buying all of the latest and greatest gadgets when they hit the market with the hopes they would be "the one" and suddenly solve his organization challenges. He came to realize it didn't have anything to do the gadgets them-selves, but instead the fact that he hadn't developed the habits to incorporate them successfully into his work practices.

APRIL 7

Take a "Procrastination Inventory."

■ ■ ■

Do you tend to be a procrastinator? Write down the things you've been putting off. Give each item a timeframe and deadline. It's helpful to identify the tasks that are getting put off. Make a plan to address each item so that you can work towards wiping them off your list!

APRIL 8

Keep track of pending replies.

■ ■ ■

Create a "Waiting for Response" folder in your inbox mail folders to keep track of messages you are awaiting a reply on. Having a system to keep things from falling through the cracks and being forgotten is critical. It also alleviates the temptation to keep this type of information in your inbox.

APRIL 9

Recognizing your "wins" is important!

▦　　▦　　▦

Celebrate something you and/or your team succeeded at today whether it is big or small. It feels good and can inspire you to stick with the more difficult projects. Celebrating a job well done is fun, too!

APRIL 10

Reduce distractions for effective
face-to-face time.

■   ■   ■

When someone comes by your desk to talk, turn off your computer monitor, close the project folder you are working on, or bookmark a page in a book so you can give them your full attention. It's easy to get distracted by stimuli in your environment when you are talking with people. It's most productive and respectful to be fully focused on them by reducing distractions.

APRIL 11

Start planning your summer vacation in advance.

■　　■　　■

Summer is a busy time to get away. Make your plans in advance so you are sure to get the campground, hotel or reservation of your choice. Keep important information related to your time away in a centralized place so planning doesn't turn into a chore and you can enjoy the process.

APRIL 12

Delete or archive emails related to completed projects.

■ ■ ■

Once you complete a project, either delete the corresponding email folder and its contents or consider moving the contents to My Documents or the network drive. You no longer need easy access to those emails (if you need them at all). Move them to a location where you can access them again if needed.

APRIL 13

* * *

All of us are stars and deserve the right to twinkle.

– Marilyn Monroe

APRIL 14

Schedule recurring tasks on your calendar or task list.

■　■　■

By using your calendar or task list, you can schedule repetitive activities and not worry about forgetting about them. It lightens the load on your memory by not having to remember them, and is a relief to not experience the "Oops—I forgot!" situations.

APRIL 15

*Give people your
undivided attention.*

■   ■   ■

Relationships are important. People deserve
your full attention. Not only does this make them
feel important, but it will also make you feel
good, too, knowing they were your sole focus. Be
so attentive that if you were asked at the end of
your interaction to summarize your
conversation, you could do it.

APRIL 16

Block time on your schedule to plan in advance for upcoming meetings and presentations.

◾ ◾ ◾

There's nothing worse than scrambling at the last minute and doing a poor job because you didn't take the time to prepare.

APRIL 17

To minimize phone tag today, leave detailed messages for people you are trying to reach.

※　　※　　※

Ask precise questions, leave specific details or provide options that can be specifically responded to in your voicemail messages. The recipient can provide you the information you need if you provide them specific requests and important details.

APRIL 18

Clean up and organize your email folders.

■ ▓ ▓

Most people have more email folders than they need. Review the folders you have. Which can you delete or archive?

APRIL 19

*Focus on the important
vs. the urgent today.*

◼   ◼   ◼

It's easy to confuse important and urgent. To
get the best results in your day, spend time completing important tasks as they relate to the
goals you are trying to achieve. Urgency needs to
be considered cautiously. Just because something is urgent doesn't mean it's important.

APRIL 20

Lesson Learned:

■　■　■

A man found that if he took a short break every hour it re-energized him and helped him be productive. He began setting a timer on an hourly basis and would walk the three flights of stairs in the building. Exercised and energized!

APRIL 21

As you do your work today, be mindful that you are spending your time on high-value activities.

▓   ▓   ▓

If you find yourself stressed, you may also find yourself spending time on low-value activities. Stay focused so you can feel productive at the end of the day and go home on time.

APRIL 22

*Use directives to clarify
the purpose of your email.*

■   ■   ■

Indicators such as FYI, URGENT, REQUEST, QUESTION, etc. in the subject line of your email provide the recipient an idea of the content of your email. These directives can also help clarify any necessary responses.

APRIL 23

Finish your meetings
with a clear action plan.

▦　　▦　　▦

If you facilitate a meeting, whether it's with just
one co-worker, your team or your entire
organization, establish a clear plan moving
forward. Define action items, who is responsible
and timeframes, all of which will be followed up
at the next session. Having a plan of action will
result in a better outcome.

APRIL 24

Take care of you!

■　■　■

Make an effort to live a healthy lifestyle: eat healthy foods, starting with a good breakfast, and drink plenty of water. Good nutrition is a key variable for having plenty of energy. Remember to keep healthy snacks at work. Fueling your body with healthy food will help you be more productive.

APRIL 25

*Purge your paper files on
a regular basis.*

▨　　▨　　▨

Are your paper file drawers overstuffed? Pull a
handful of folders every day, starting today and
purge them! Files need attention on a regular
basis. A helpful strategy is to take a moment to
review any file that you are inserting a document
into. Purge as you go!

APRIL 26

*Don't clutter your email folders
with information you
rarely need to access.*

■   ■   ■

If you have received emails that are reference information, save them in one of two locations: your email folders for information that you may need to actively use, or your My Documents or the network drive for information that is more archival. Accessibility will help you determine in which location to store your information.

APRIL 27

■ ■ ■

How we spend our days is, of course, how we spend our lives.

—*Annie Dillard*

APRIL 28

*Make good choices when you
are interrupted today.*

■　　■　　■

Interruptions are to be expected. Sometimes you
have time to allow for them. Create back up
responses for when you need to keep focused.
Schedule an appointment to follow up, ask
someone to send an email with their question or
request they return in a specific amount of time
once you've completed your current task. Set
boundaries in a respectful manner.

APRIL 29

Designate a reading area and keep your reading materials there.

■   ■   ■

Having a reading "zone" gives you a location to put your magazines, journals, catalogs and books so they are there when you want to relax and read. It also gives those publications a home so they don't drift everywhere.

APRIL 30

Find a different location to do your work from time to time.

■　■　■

To maximize work time, move to another office, conference room or even work at home or at the local coffee shop. You'll be able to minimize interruptions and accomplish more.

MAY 1

*Spend time today doing something
you are passionate about!*

▨　　▨　　▨

Engaging in your passions brings joy and happiness. Doing these things can often be what gets
dropped off your calendar when you are busy.
Make them a priority.

MAY 2

Become more proficient at using your email program.

■　■　■

Enroll in a class to improve your knowledge of your email program if you know you are just scratching the surface with your skills. Most email programs have much more depth than people have knowledge of. There are plenty of ways to sharpen your skills which will improve your productivity, save you time and help you avoid aggravation.

MAY 3

*Review your meeting
schedule today.*

■   ■   ■

Are the meetings you are scheduled to attend
important? Today's business world is meeting
crazed! Make the most of your time by only
attending those that are important for you and
that you are an asset to. (If you decide to bow
out of a meeting, be sure to let the organizer
know you won't be attending.)

MAY 4

Lesson Learned:

■ ■ ■

Desperately wanting to get his office cleaned up, a business owner paid his two children to help him. He sorted through paper and clutter and they took care of managing the recycling, shredding and garbage! They had fun doing it together. The kids now have a sense of ownership in Dad's clean office, and Dad has kids nagging him if it starts to get cluttered again!

MAY 5

*Think twice before you hit
"Reply to All" when you are
responding to emails today.*

▨   ▨   ▨

Does everyone need to receive your reply or just
the sender? Help to create a culture of "less is
more" when it comes to email by thoughtfully
considering who should receive each message.

MAY 6

*Develop an index for
your file system.*

■　■　■

Keep it accessible on your computer desktop
and/or in the front of your file drawer. This is
a helpful shortcut when you are deciding where
to file a document or where to search for one!
It takes away the guesswork.

MAY 7

Evaluate your work space.
Do you feel good here?

▨   ▨   ▨

Take a moment today to look around your work space. You spend a lot of time here. It's important that you are happy in your space. If you need to declutter to feel better, schedule time to do that. If you need to put a few special things up on your walls (photos, artwork, etc.) to inspire you, do what will make your space feel good!

MAY 8

*Develop and follow a
morning routine.*

■   ■   ■

BEFORE you dive into your inbox, have a routine
that gets your day off to a productive start. Check
your calendar, tickler file or task list and prioritize the action items on it. When creating a new
routine, consider writing it down and putting it
somewhere you will see it each morning to keep
you on track until it becomes a habit.

MAY 9

*Schedule a "re-entry" day
after your vacation.*

▦　▦　▦

When blocking vacation time on your calendar,
be proactive and plan some recovery time on the
back end. Don't schedule meetings the day you
return. Give yourself some recuperation and
catch up time so that you can hold onto that
calm, relaxed feeling for as long as possible!

MAY 10

*Break down big projects
into smaller steps.*

■　■　■

When you take on a new project, big or small,
be sure to break it down into individual action
items and put them on your calendar or to-do
list. It's easy to think of a project as one large
action, when actually most projects are a series
of smaller to-do's. Create a list, table or spreadsheet of the action items and their order from
beginning to end including deadlines.

MAY 11

░ ░ ░

Today should always be
our most wonderful day.

— *Thomas Dreir*

MAY 12

*Provide detail yet be succinct
in the subject line of emails.*

■　　■　　■

Your recipients are much more likely to read
your email if they have a good idea of what the
email is about. Your subject line should contain
key words that will help the reader understand
the topic of the email.

MAY 13

*Utilize an action system that
supports recurring activities.*

▨ ▨ ▨

Know that the next time your monthly mileage
report is due, or your business partner's birth-
day comes, those things won't fall through the
cracks. Whether it's recording those dates in a
paper tickler system or an electronic task
system, you can rest assured they won't be
forgotten!

MAY 14

When planning a vacation, create a checklist for the things you need to take care of at the office.

■   ■   ■

Why reinvent the wheel every time you go on vacation and take the risk of forgetting something important? Create a checklist you can reuse each time you are planning time away to make sure all your bases are covered.

MAY 15

Creating new habits takes time, commitment, repetition and discipline. Be gentle with yourself!

■ ■ ■

Whether you are on a new exercise program, trying a new diet, working on becoming more organized, or implementing new strategies to take control of your email, it's a process and doesn't happen overnight. Allow yourself time to develop these new patterns and celebrate your successes.

MAY 16

Energy is critical to your success.

■ ■ ■

Managing your energy can be just as important
as managing your time, your email and other
processes in your day. It is needed to lead,
inspire and make a difference. Be mindful to fill
your day with things that energize you, naturally.

MAY 17

Evaluate how you spend your time.

▦ ▦ ▦

Are you truly as busy as you think you are? To find out where your time REALLY goes, consider doing a time study for 3-5 days. Print a calendar that has your work hours listed in 10-15 minute increments. List what you do during those time blocks. It's helpful to know how much of your time is being spent on meaningful work activity and how much is being wasted with low value tasks. Make the shifts you need to!

MAY 18

Lesson Learned:

■　■　■

Instead of coming back from meetings with
pages of notes interspersed with action items
(that would eventually often get overlooked),
a manager now takes her project folder and a
stack of capture cards to meetings. She records
her general notes in her project folder and
returns to her office with action items on capture
cards and places them in her action system.

MAY 19

Take a technology vacation today!

▨ ▨ ▨

Getting away from your computer, cell phone
and any other technology is incredibly refreshing. Even if it's just for an hour or even 30
minutes, enjoy some off-line time. Turn it off —
you really can do it!

MAY 20

Plan ahead for more productive appointments and meetings.

■　■　■

Take time today to prepare for the clients and meetings you have tomorrow. Develop agendas, create notes, prepare materials, etc. Waiting until the day of your meetings to prepare can cause a lot of stress. Sometimes it can mean not having the information or products available that you need. Always be looking ahead to have ample time to plan.

MAY 21

Label your paper files using large, bold print or a felt tip marker.

■   ■   ■

The file system is *your* system. Be sure to create file names that are meaningful to you. It's important to be able to read the names of your folders easily and find what you are looking for. Create an index to help you find files quickly.

MAY 22

*Block time for yourself this week
to catch up on your reading.*

■   ■   ■

Keeping your mind sharp and learning more
about your community, your world and your
profession is a key part of your success. There is
a lot of information that needs to be read—
books, articles, newsletters, etc. They add up and
need regular time on your calendar. If possible,
treat yourself and get out of the office to do it!

MAY 23

Keep your calendar current.

※　※　※

When you receive information about an event or meeting via email, move it immediately onto your calendar. Don't miss an event because you left the information sitting in your inbox!

MAY 24

Time can seem to fly by!
Take note of what you do today.

■   ■   ■

If you often get to the end of the day and wonder,
"Yikes! Where did the day go?" take a moment to
reflect on all the things that transpired in your
day. Not only will it help you appreciate all you
did, but it will also help your memory retain
those activities after the fact.

▦ ▦ ▦

Few things are impossible to diligence and skill. Great works are performed not by strength, but perseverance. — Samuel Johnson

MAY 26

Reorganize dysfunctional areas in your workspace.

■   ■   ■

The most functional work area has the items that are used frequently in locations with easy accessibility. The things used less often can be stored on the perimeter. Think about your desk—your phone, computer and project files are close at hand. Reference information that is only used on occasion can be stored away from your desk.

MAY 27

*Reward yourself for completing
the tough stuff.*

▓   ▓   ▓

When you are facing a task or activity that you
aren't looking forward to today, plan to reward
yourself with something fun when you get it
done. It can just be something small (or big, if
you'd like)—taking a short walk, getting a cup of
coffee, calling a friend, taking the afternoon off.
Give yourself kudos for completing the task.

MAY 28

Unsubscribe from mailing lists of publications you no longer want.

■   ■   ■

It only takes a few seconds and in the long run will save you time by getting that unwanted email out of your inbox once and for all. Contact organizations that send print publication to be removed from their lists.

Consider other ways of saying "NO!"

▨   ▨   ▨

Frequently people are hesitant to say NO to doing something they're asked to do. If you truly don't have the time and energy to give something your all, it's important to let the person know you will not be able to complete the task or project with the best quality. With that in mind, you may not be the best choice for the job (at this time). If it's a project at work, consider if there is something on your plate that could be shifted to someone else to enable you to take on the new project.

MAY 30

What activities energize you,
naturally?

■　■　■

Being aware of activities you can do that bring
you energy without having to depend on
artificial energy sources (Rockstar, 5 Hour
Energy, Starbucks, etc.) is invaluable. What
habits might need to be changed so you can find
energy in natural ways?

MAY 31

Think outside the box and make your contact manager an even more powerful tool!

▧　▧　▧

Use your contact management system to keep track of information beyond the traditional name, phone number, email and address. Utilize it to track resource information such as account numbers, membership numbers, usernames and passwords, etc.

JUNE 1

Lesson Learned:

■　　■　　■

Two co-workers became tremendous accountability partners. They met twice a month and compared notes on their path to becoming more productive. Their encouragement produced positive results—they both got promotions!

JUNE 2

*If you struggle with wanting
things to be perfect,
set time limits for tasks.*

▨   ▨   ▨

"Done is better than perfect!" is a well-known
mantra among perfectionists. Pursue doing
things well, but don't get stuck on getting them
perfect—you'll never get things done and you'll
become frustrated along the way.

JUNE 3

Leave an "out of office" message
when you are on vacation.

■   ■   ■

Remember to leave a message on your voicemail
as well as an auto-responder on your email,
letting people know you are out of the office and
when you'll return. Let them know you are
unavailable and who they can contact for urgent
issues. Enjoy your time away without feeling you
need to respond to messages. If people have the
expectation you won't be returning messages
right away, you don't have to worry about follow
up until you return to work.

JUNE 4

Make time to exercise every day.

▪   ▪   ▪

Whether you run, bike, work out at the gym, or walk 15-20 minutes a day, make exercise a priority. You'll be more energized and conse-quently, more productive.

JUNE 5

Keep your calendar or task list on your computer screen instead of your inbox.

■　■　■

This practice will allow you to be more focused on your work and less distracted by email. Eliminate the temptation of getting sucked into your inbox when there are other tasks needing to be accomplished.

JUNE 6

Does your work space have visual appeal?

■   ■   ■

Look around your work space. "Visual clutter" can be a stumbling block in your productivity. If you've got extraneous "stuff" on your walls (phone numbers, account numbers, old cartoons, etc.) toss what you don't need and put the things you frequently use in an easy to access file folder or binder. Consider putting up a photo or two, or some artwork that inspires you and will make you feel happy.

JUNE 7

Exercise calendar control—
don't overschedule yourself!

■   ■   ■

Avoid scheduling yourself in back-to-back
meetings and appointments. That invites burn
out and overwhelm. Allow for breaks (even short
ones) in between meetings and appointments.

JUNE 8

■ ■ ■

It is always the simple
that produces the marvelous.

— Amelia Barr

JUNE 9

Prepare adequate coverage for your vacations and times away from the office.

■　■　■

If you are planning time away from the office for vacation, make sure co-workers have what they need to cover for you and to follow up on projects while you are gone. With good planning and communication, you'll be able to minimize any hiccups so you can relax during your vacation, knowing things at the office are in good hands.

JUNE 10

*Be on time for meetings
and appointments.*

▦　　▦　　▦

When it's time to leave to attend an appointment
or meeting, GO! Don't try to squeeze in just one
more task. It's more important to be on time or
early. That task will be there when you return.
Bask in the joy of being on time!

JUNE 11

*Create "power folders" for
digital information you save
on a regular basis.*

■　■　■

If you have multiple clients, customers, vendors,
etc. whose information you like to have arranged
in the same format, creating a power folder
allows you to design a format, then easily repro-
duce it for any new entry.

JUNE 12

*Strive to be a positive influence
on the people around you.*

▩　▩　▩

It's a compliment when you are an inspiration
and people want to do whatever they can to be
with you. Find ways to encourage and support
others at work and in other areas of your life.

JUNE 13

*Are you aware of your
team, department
or organization's goals?*

■ ■ ■

It's important to have short-term and long-term
goals in order to have a clear direction. Be
proactive in reviewing them on a regular basis
and keeping them up to date.

JUNE 14

*Make a plan before you leave
to run errands.*

▨　▨　▨

Determine what it is you need to do while you
are out and about. Map out your stops so you are
efficient with your time. Keep a list of each stop
and anything you require for completing the
errands. Be sure to review the list before you
leave the office to be sure you have everything
you need.

JUNE 15

Lesson Learned:

■   ■   ■

Capture Cards became such a mainstay in one office that they, along with pens, can now be found in every conference room in a stylish container. Employees can record their thoughts and ideas during meetings and are able to return their focus back to the discussion quickly and without losing momentum.

JUNE 16

*When using technology at meetings,
keep focused and stay on task.*

◼   ◼   ◼

If you use a laptop or tablet at meetings and
presentations to take notes, be disciplined to
ONLY have your notes program or app running.
You've made a commitment of your time when
you attend events. Be fully present—don't
distract yourself by checking email, social media
or surfing the web. It's also disrespectful to the
speaker, meeting planner and other participants.

JUNE 17

Filter your task list or action file of unimportant, low value, "busy work" tasks today.

■   ■   ■

There are only so many hours in the day. At one time, some of your "to do's" may have been valuable, yet as time moves on there may be a shift. Get rid of those that truly no longer matter.

JUNE 18

Set clear boundaries if you need to work while on vacation.

▨ ▨ ▨

If checking business email or phone messages is critical when you are on vacation this summer, set clear limits and time frames for having your work hat on. Allow yourself time to stay connected, but remember, vacation is your time to refuel!

*Connect with others who have
skills you aspire to.*

■ ■ ■

Identify someone who is more advanced in your
field than you are. Call them and ask them to
meet for coffee or lunch. Go prepared with
questions to make the best use of your time
together. Hanging around people who are more
skilled than you are can only make you better!

JUNE 20

Be proactive with the meetings you attend.

▩　▩　▩

Request an agenda in advance. A large number of meetings lack objectives and an agenda. It can be easy to get off track in these meetings and feel like time is wasted. Meetings with agendas are more productive and more enjoyable!

JUNE 21

Spend time doing what you are passionate about!

▧ ▧ ▧

Say NO to Facebook and TV. The average American spends more than 11 hours per month on Facebook and watches 38.5 hours of television per week. Take back your time and do something you really love!

▓ ▓ ▓

We can easily manage if we will only take, each day, the burden appointed to it. But the load will be too heavy for us if we carry yesterday's burden over again today, and then add the burden of the morrow before we are required to bear it. — *John Newton*

JUNE 23

*Take control of making
the most of your time!*

■　■　■

Look at your calendar today. Is there anything on
it that is unnecessary for you to attend? Be
assertive and proactive in cutting things out of
your schedule. Practice good choice
management.

JUNE 24

*Plan ahead to be productive
when you travel.*

▓   ▓   ▓

If you head off on a business trip, be sure to have
your tasks with you that you need to accomplish
while you are on the road. Take any ancillary
information with you that you might need. Be
prepared with the resources you need to
accomplish your work, even when you are out of
the office.

JUNE 25

Assess your physical, mental, emotional and spiritual energy.

▨   ▨   ▨

How is your energy today? Energy is a critical resource. It's important to have an awareness of your energy so that you have enough to execute the important stuff in your day.

JUNE 26

Check your calendar today
for upcoming projects.

▓   ▓   ▓

If you have an upcoming deadline for a project or
task, be sure you plan far enough out on your
calendar to do the work. On your calendar or
task list, write the date you want to START
working on the task, not just the due date to
ensure it will be completed on time.

JUNE 27

*Process the email in your inbox
with the intention of getting
it out of your inbox.*

■　■　■

Make an immediate decision about each email as
you process it—either **delete** it if it's unimportant, **forward** it if it's pertinent or a task to
delegate to someone else; **reply** if it's something
you can take care of quickly (in 1-2 minutes);
save it to a file or email folder if it will be needed
in the future or, **move it** to your calendar, task
list or to-do list if it needs action later on. It feels
SO good to take control of your inbox!

JUNE 28

Create a project plan in either written or electronic format for all your projects, large or small.

▨ ▨ ▨

Keeping a copy of the project plan with the corresponding documentation will help you manage the project more successfully.

JUNE 29

Lesson Learned:

■ ■ ■

A busy entrepreneur realized she needed to get some help in designing a file system for her business when she discovered she'd leave faxes in the fax machine because if she removed them she might never find them again.

JUNE 30

Whatever you do today,
be "in the moment!"

※　※　※

It's easy to operate as if you're on auto pilot and
not really aware of what you are doing. Have you
ever gotten to the end of a day and wondered,
"What did I do today?" Practice the habit of being
in the moment!

JULY 1

Schedule a date with yourself to do a quarterly review of your goals.

■ ■ ■

Do a progress check and update your goals accordingly. To achieve success, goals need to be assessed and re-assessed. And what a great opportunity to see the progress you've made!

JULY 2

Pay attention to how much you interrupt other people.

■　■　■

It's one thing to get interrupted yourself and another thing when you are the interrupter! Make an effort to respect other people's time. Can you email a question if it doesn't need an immediate answer? Keep a list of multiple items for one person so you can take care of all your requests in one interaction.

JULY 3

Develop a plan for your day today.

■ ■ ■

Many people think they are too busy to plan, but diving into your day without a plan of action is like taking a road trip without a map. Who knows if you'll get lost and if you'll arrive at your destination! Take the first 10 minutes of your day to create your game plan (if you didn't already do it before leaving work last night).

JULY 4

Do your best to find the positives today. Be enthusiastic about the things you do.

■ ■ ■

Seeing the glass half full instead of half empty is a much happier attitude to have as you go through your day—whether it's at work or outside of work. Look for the good around you and be mindful of how a positive attitude can help you be successful.

JULY 5

Create calendar events for important activities and commitments.

■　■　■

It's essential to honor your own needs and commitments. Whether it's completing a project to meet a deadline, creating your daily action plan or getting yourself to the gym, set an appointment with yourself to make sure these important tasks get done.

■ ■ ■

In the long run, we shape our lives,
and we shape ourselves.
The process never ends until we die.
And the choices we make are
ultimately our own responsibility.

— *Eleanor Roosevelt*

JULY 7

If you tend to be a procrastinator, identify some of your avoidance activities.

■   ■   ■

Common ones are: hiding out in your inbox, texting, chit-chatting at the office, and working on low-value tasks. Knowing what your avoidance tendencies are can help you recognize when you may be procrastinating. When you notice that "ah-ha," dive in and just do it!

JULY 8

Utilize the three volley email rule.

■　■　■

Are there any conversations that have been volleying back and forth unnecessarily in your inbox? If so, call the sender, or send a request to schedule a meeting or phone call to complete the discussion. After a message volleys back and forth three times, it's time to talk! Time can be wasted by multiple emails that could be taken care of in a single discussion.

JULY 9

*Carry reading materials with you
when you're on the go.*

■　■　■

Who knows when you'll arrive at a meeting
early, or have to wait in a doctor's office, or have
time sitting in the car while your child's ballet
class gets done. If you've got a portable folder of
articles, magazines, catalogs that you want to
read, you can indulge yourself! (You can also
pre-load documents and articles on your smart
phone or tablet for reading on the go.)

JULY 10

If you succeed at implementing a new habit today, reward yourself!

■ ■ ■

Sometimes it's easy to focus on all the things we want to improve or change. Don't forget to celebrate your successes. If you are seeing progress in an area you are working on, do something special and fun!

JULY 11

*Take 10 minutes today to
tidy up and organize
an area you use frequently.*

◼   ◼   ◼

Do this with your desktop, your "junk drawer,"
your computer desktop, etc. Consider doing it
every day. Organizing the space around you
doesn't necessarily need to be done all at once.
Break it into small, manageable pieces. You can
accomplish a lot in 10 minutes!

JULY 12

Enjoy your people time.
Take a technology break.

■   ■   ■

Technology has a way of monopolizing time spent with people. When attending social events, whether business or personal, make the most of the time you have together and resist the urge to constantly reach for your device. Put cell phones on silent and try to put them in a bag or pocket you won't constantly be checking. Remember – all the messages, emails and voicemails will be there waiting for you after the event, and you'll have more fun!

JULY 13

Lesson Learned:

■   ■   ■

An employee who works with a very close team implemented a number of productivity strate-gies and suddenly was early meeting deadlines, had a tidy desk, and had a new sense of calm about her. Many of her co-workers started spending time around her in order to pick up on her new ways.

JULY 14

*Find a different place to eat
besides at your desk.*

■   ■   ■

Eat lunch somewhere else than at your desk or
at the office today. If the weather is decent,
include a walk around the block. Taking a break
and getting a change of scenery is critical to
performing your best. You'll be re-energized for
what's on your agenda in the afternoon.

Consider holding "stand up meetings" to keep meetings brief.

▨　▨　▨

If having regular meetings is necessary for you and your team or department, consider holding stand up meetings where people make brief reports. The purpose behind this type of meeting is being concise and to the point. People tend to keep things short and sweet if they can't get too comfortable!

JULY 16

Evaluate your workspace to be sure it is situated so you can work most effectively.

■   ■   ■

Look at how your desk is positioned—do you face the door? This may be a cause for lots of distractions when people walk by. Think strategically about where you place furnishings and resources you use every day and how they can impact your work flow.

JULY 17

Limit your number of email folders.

■   ■   ■

If you have too many folders in your inbox, consider simply creating a folder for the year, or
possibly each quarter of the year where you can
save emails and use the search feature to find
them. Having too many folders can cause wasted
time by scrolling up and down. The search
feature is a powerful tool!

JULY 18

*Be aware of the choices you make
with your time today.*

■ ■ ■

Your time is a finite resource. Making the most of
it is a constant balancing act throughout the day.
No matter what you choose to do, remind
yourself of two facts: first, by saying YES to doing
something, you are saying NO to something else;
and second, is just the opposite—saying NO to
something means you have the freedom to say
YES to something else!

*Finish one task, or get to
a good stopping place,
before you dive into another.*

■　■　■

With all the things you may have on your to-do
list, it's easy to want to be working on several at
once. Know that you are most efficient when you
focus on one thing at a time. It may be a challenge, but try it and you'll see. It's also much less
stressful!

▨ ▨ ▨

You may delay, but time will not,

and lost time is never found again.

— *Benjamin Franklin*

JULY 21

Seek help in prioritizing.

■ ■ ■

If you need help figuring out how to juggle all the projects and tasks on your plate, or how to prioritize them, ask for input from your supervisor. When everything seems important or when you feel overwhelmed with your projects and tasks, your supervisor may be best to help you clarify. Checking in on a regular basis will help ensure you are on the same page with what needs to be done first.

JULY 22

*Take short breaks
throughout your day.*

■ ■ ■

Take breaks during your day, or better yet, even
a nap! If it helps, set a timer or alarm to remind
you. Taking a time out every 60-90 minutes will
refresh you and you will be better able to focus,
resulting in higher quality work. Often, it's when
we need it most that we are least apt to make the
time for a break!

JULY 23

*Utilize technology to send
yourself important reminders.*

■   ■   ■

If it's not convenient to write yourself a note or
you don't have paper and pen and you need to
remember something important, call yourself
and leave a message or send yourself an email so
you can let go of worrying about remembering it!

JULY 24

*Give your paper
files expiration dates.*

■　■　■

If a document you are filing will be obsolete on a certain date, write that date on top of the piece of paper. Being able to easily see a "toss by date" on a document makes it easy to discard without having to review it.

*Think twice before you hit "save" on
emails or electronic documents.*

▪   ▪   ▪

Electronic communication and documents are
invisible in a sense. It's easy to save things you'll
never access again. (Eighty percent of what
people save is never looked at again!) Do
yourself the favor of being selective in what you
save and avoid large purging projects in the
future that come from saving too much.

JULY 26

Go out of your way to do something special for someone today!

※　※　※

Pick up the phone and call someone you haven't spoken to in a while, leave someone a thoughtful note, have lunch with a friend, or surprise someone with something fun. Big or small, it will make both of you feel good!

Lesson Learned:

▨   ▨   ▨

A manager found freedom in unsubscribing from publications and newsletters she just didn't have time to read. She realized that in this information age she needed to be realistic about the time she has to read, and selective about what public-cations were most valuable and let go of the rest.

JULY 28

Schedule "Focus Time"
for yourself daily.

■　■　■

Block a chunk or two of uninterrupted time
during your day (a minimum of 30 minutes at
a time) to work on your most important tasks.
Close your door, turn off your cell phone, set
your landline to "do not disturb" and turn off
email notifiers. You'll be amazed at how much
you are able to accomplish.

JULY 29

When you are developing a project plan, always ask yourself, "What's the next step?"

■ ■ ■

When you take on a project, it's easy to jump all over the map if you don't have a plan. Often you may jump ahead several steps not realizing an action item may have dependencies of its own that need to be taken care of.

JULY 30

Reflect on the interruptions you experience on a regular basis.

■ ■ ■

Think about ways you can be proactive to lessen their frequency. Interruptions are to be expected but those that happen routinely have a big impact on your productivity.

JULY 31

Respond to your voicemail
on a regular basis.

■　■　■

Keep on top of your voicemail box. Just as with paper or electronic information, make a decision about each message—delete it if it's not important, take care of it right away or add it to your task list and then delete it. Avoid the habit of saving to-do's on your voicemail.

AUGUST 1

Resist the temptation to dive into small, low value tasks first today.

■   ■   ■

Keep working on developing the habit to discipline yourself to take on your most important thing! Low value tasks may be easy but they won't move you toward your overall goals.

AUGUST 2

Practice gratitude with others.

▓ ▓ ▓

Take a moment to say "Thank you!" to someone today, whether it's via a phone call, an email, a text or even an old fashioned, handwritten note. It can be easier sometimes to notice what's wrong instead of celebrating what's right… Recognizing the good is good!

AUGUST 3

■ ■ ■

I long to accomplish a great and noble task, but it is my chief duty to accomplish small tasks as if they were great and noble. — *Helen Keller*

AUGUST 4

*Be realistic about your
to-do list today.*

▪ ▪ ▪

Consider the activities you have on your calendar today along with your energy as you determine what to commit yourself to today. It's all too easy at the beginning of the day to create a long to-do list when it's just not realistic. Be realistic so that you can feel good about what you DID accomplish at the end of the day, not frustrated about the things you never got done.

AUGUST 5

Include a date in the subject line of an email if there is a timeframe or deadline for a response.

■   ■   ■

Your recipient will be alerted that they need to address your email in a timely fashion since it is time sensitive.

AUGUST 6

Stock up on supplies.

■　■　■

Check to be sure you have what you need in your office that allows you to do your job most effectively. If you find yourself constantly going to the supply room or office store for things you use frequently, get a large supply and store it somewhere convenient in your office to avoid wasting valuable time chasing down supplies. (Think about printer paper, file folders, post-it notes, pads, envelopes, etc.)

AUGUST 7

Use recycled products and reuse supplies when you have the option.

■ ■ ■

Make good choices that will help minimize clutter in the office, save money and help protect the environment.

AUGUST 8

Find a happy medium when it comes to being social at the office.

■   ■   ■

Consider ways you can socialize in a productive way: taking walks with co-workers, having lunch together, etc. People are important and building relationships with your colleagues is vital to having a positive work environment. Know when it's time to get back to work!

AUGUST 9

Develop a system for dumping your mental clutter!

■   ■   ■

There is only so much room in your brain for information. In an effort to keep your brain free for the information that is important, develop a strategy to capture the mental clutter that can get in the way. Choose a medium that works for you: index cards, a notepad, or an electronic device. Take a moment to jot down the thoughts that enter your mind so that you can be fully present with the task at hand. Keep that capture medium nearby at all times and when time permits, transfer these thoughts and tasks to your calendar or task list.

Lesson Learned:

■ ■ ■

A high level manager thought she had control of her office even though it was covered with stacks of paper everywhere. "I know where everything is!" Until one day when the CEO arrived at her door and asked about one of the projects she was working on. Embarrassingly enough, she wasn't able to find the file. A well designed file system was quickly developed and now she operates more efficiently than she ever realized she could.

AUGUST 11

Determine if you are
well-matched for your job.

■ ■ ■

If you are, celebrate YOU! If not, can you delegate
the parts that aren't a good match? Or can you
renegotiate some of your job responsibilities?
People are happiest and most productive when
their personalities are matched with the work
they do.

AUGUST 12

Evaluate the true productivity
of your technology.

■　■　■

Take note of the various gadgets you have surrounded yourself with. Not all gadgets work for all people. It's an individual preference. Do your devices help you or hinder you? Make adjustments to the technology you utilize if you need to. Sometimes, simpler is better.

AUGUST 13

Do a happiness check today
at work.

▩ ▩ ▩

How happy are you? How much joy does your
work bring you? Is it a "j-o-b" or is it something
you do with passion and joy? If you are not as
happy as you'd like, what adjustments can you
make to find the level of happiness you deserve?
A lot of life is spent at work; be happy doing it!

AUGUST 14

Set a timer or alarm for yourself to keep on task.

■   ■   ■

This strategy alleviates the disruption of constantly looking at the clock. You can put your head down and work hard, knowing the timer or alarm will let you know when it's quitting time!

AUGUST 15

Maintain good work boundaries.

■　■　■

Life-work balance — it's a daily work in progress. Do your best to draw boundaries separating work from the time you have with your friends and family. Being fully present with the people in your life is important for everyone. If you need to work at home, designate specific times to do it and let everyone know when you'll have your work hat on and when you'll be free to have fun and play.

AUGUST 16

Are you happy with the calendar or schedule system you are using?

■　　■　　■

If not, look at other options. Keeping an up-to-date calendar is critical for making the most of your time. Don't hesitate to change systems if what you are using isn't working. Consider paper and electronic options. There are plenty of good ones available.

■ ▓ ▓

By failing to prepare,

you are preparing to fail.

— *Benjamin Franklin*

AUGUST 18

Use your contact manager to keep track of valuable information.

■   ■   ■

Keep notes in your contact manager of personal things a connection may have shared with you as you build working relationships. You can be reminded of these the next time you talk and ask for updates. This shows that you are not only concerned about your business relationship, but that you have a personal interest as well.

AUGUST 19

Set time limits on meeting agenda items.

※　※　※

When preparing meeting agendas, list a time frame next to each item. Request that speakers limit their comments and reports to the allotted time. Keeping meetings moving along will be easier if people are aware of the schedule and time limitations.

AUGUST 20

Create a consistent format for naming your digital documents.

■　■　■

Consider using key pieces of information such as the date and name of project as well as any version number information that will help to keep files organized. Consistency makes retrieving documents much easier.

AUGUST 21

Make good choices about how you spend your time today.

▩ ▩ ▩

Remember that how you spend your time is a matter of the CHOICES you make. If you are feeling like time is out of control, step back, take a deep breath and take control of what you want to use your time for. YOU really are in control of your time!

AUGUST 22

Delegate, delegate, delegate!

▓   ▓   ▓

If there are tasks or projects you need help with, seek someone out. Or maybe there is someone that is better skilled and would be a more appropriate fit to take over the job. Don't be shy!

AUGUST 23

*Prioritize where you will invest
your energy today.*

◾ ◾ ◾

Be realistic about the things you will need
energy for today. At some point, your energy will
run out. Remember your priorities (your goals
and your three "must do's" for today). Even
though you can refuel your energy during the
day, there is a limit. Do your best to expend
energy on the things you can control.

AUGUST 24

Lesson Learned:

■　■　■

An employee had a huge "ah ha" moment about email distraction once he found out just how much more productive he was when he minimized his email on his computer screen. He is committed to his new mantra: "Minimize email!" What a difference it has made!

Create a rule in your email for something that would save you time.

▨   ▨   ▨

Rules can be set up for items that you want to bypass your inbox, for things you want to go directly to your junk or deleted folder, and many more options. If you are unfamiliar with how to create rules, take a few minutes to learn how. They can be a huge time saver!

*Develop the mindset of
daily purging.*

■ ■ ■

Put a box in the corner of your workspace. Every
day, put something in the box that you no longer
use or need. At the end of the week, recycle,
shred or donate the contents. Decluttering your
workspace will improve your workflow and your
ability to focus.

AUGUST 27

Review where you store different forms of paper documents.

■　　■　　■

They should be kept in locations determined by the frequency of access. Action files and project files which get used on a regular basis should reside in a location close to you with easy access. Reference and archive files can live somewhere less convenient and accessible.

AUGUST 28

Do your best today to be aware of interrupting yourself.

■　■　■

Fight the temptation to switch your attention from something you are working on to check your Facebook page or texting a friend. You already face enough external interruptions that you may not have control over. Take control of your "self- interruptions." You can do it!

Before you take on any new projects today, think about what's already on your plate.

▪ ▪ ▪

It's so easy to say, "YES!" to new projects. Get in the habit of stepping back and taking inventory of what's occupying your time. Ask yourself if you truly can handle taking on something else. Learn to say "NO!" when it's appropriate.

AUGUST 30

Learn shortcuts to save time with email and other programs.

■　■　■

There are many shortcuts available for the electronic and email programs you use. Some people are avid shortcut users others just have a few favorites. Determine what works best for you. If it helps, keep keyboard lists nearby and learn one new shortcut a day.

■ ■ ■

Happiness is not optional.

Happiness is not for the few,

or the lucky, or for those

who are "deserving."

Happiness is mandatory,

as important as air,

as food and water.

Happiness is our birthright.

– Kellie Poulsen-Grill

SEPTEMBER 1

Start and end meetings on time.

■   ■   ■

If you facilitate a meeting, whether it's with just one co-worker, your team or your entire organization, be adamant about starting and finishing on time. Respect the schedules of those who are in attendance at your meeting. Their time, as well as yours, is valuable!

SEPTEMBER 2

*Becoming more organized
is primarily about developing
good habits.*

■   ■   ■

What is a new or recently adopted habit that you want to focus on today? Time and repetition are critical for a new habit to become a way of life. You'll be one day closer after today.

SEPTEMBER 3

*Find natural ways to renew
your energy.*

■　　■　　■

Not every day goes as planned. Sometimes crises
can be anticipated, other times they happen
unexpectedly. Be prepared either way. If you hit
the wall today energy-wise, be aware of the
things you can do to refill your tank and renew
your energy. Do it naturally if you can!

SEPTEMBER 4

Determine appropriate response times for email and voicemail.

▨　▨　▨

Determining response time expectations is valuable for you, your customers/clients and your colleagues. If you need input from your supervisor, don't hesitate to ask (you might be surprised that their expectations are less than what you think). It alleviates the unrealistic need for everything to happen NOW and will allow you to get more done!

SEPTEMBER 5

*Get rid of horizontal
organizing trays.*

■　■　■

Oftentimes, paper and files that get placed in a
horizontal organizer are never seen again and
can be a graveyard for your paper. Organize files
and paper in vertical organizers or in a file
drawer.

SEPTEMBER 6

*Review any problems you are
currently dealing with and how
you are working to resolve them.*

▨　▨　▨

Remember, you'll get the best results by either
changing something about yourself or your
environment. You have control of yourself and
your environment. Trying to change something
about someone else rarely works well.

SEPTEMBER 7

Lesson Learned:

■ ■ ■

A single mom was so thrilled with how Focus Time helped her at work that she instigated it at home with her children who had been nagging her to read to them more often. At 7:00 PM, all cell phones were turned off (hers included) and mom and the three kids had two hours of family time before bed.

SEPTEMBER 8

Craft quality emails.

■   ■   ■

As you compose emails today, make an effort to improve the readability of what you write and how you write it. Be brief, use bullet points and conclude with any action required. Eliminating lots of blah, blah, blah will be more productive for both you and your recipient. Sometimes longer emails only get scanned instead of thoroughly read and important details might be missed.

SEPTEMBER 9

*Use your action system to follow up
on delegated projects.*

■　　■　　■

Remember that when you delegate a project or
task, the final responsibility is still yours. Put a
reminder in your action system or on your task
list to contact the person you have delegated to
for a status check. Having a solid action system is
key to having consistent follow up.

*If you tend to procrastinate,
take time to reflect on why.*

■   ■   ■

Maybe you love the thrill of that adrenaline rush
when you wait to the last minute, or maybe you
have a difficult time making decisions. Maybe
you are easily overwhelmed by large projects.
Understanding the WHY is the first step to being
able to kick the procrastination habit!

SEPTEMBER 11

Set small goals to see progress.

■　■　■

If you have a new project or a new skill you are trying to learn, make progress by taking baby steps. It's so easy to want to get it done NOW! Often that's just not realistic. Make slow, steady progress and you will reach your goals.

SEPTEMBER 12

*Box up and store inactive files
or outdated information.*

▨　▨　▨

Don't fill up your work space with old information you no longer need. If you cannot toss
or recycle the documents, store them in sturdy
boxes and label them well.

SEPTEMBER 13

Turn off your monitor(s) when you are not using it or when you are meeting with someone.

■　■　■

You'll be surprised at how different your space will feel without the glare of information staring at you when you are trying to focus on a project or a person. Not having the screen "noise" is surprisingly relaxing and peaceful.

■ ■ ■

Great things are not done by impulse, but by a series of small things brought together.

— *George Eliot*

SEPTEMBER 15

Think "big picture" when you plan your day today.

▨ ▨ ▨

Determine the most important things you need to get done at work, but also consider the things that need to be accomplished in your personal life, with your family, when and how you will exercise and anything else that is critical. Instead of having a long list for each of those areas, determine the one or two most critical items that must be accomplished. As you are probably aware, it's unreasonable to do it ALL!

SEPTEMBER 16

Determine an area in which you would like to increase your knowledge and skills.

■   ■   ■

You perform best and are happiest when your knowledge and skills match the tasks you are required to perform. Make a plan toward accomplishing that goal. Take step number one today!

SEPTEMBER 17

*Make an effort to continually
refine your systems and processes.*

■   ■   ■

They will serve you well when crises occur.
There are days that, for whatever reason, get out
of control and priorities need to be reset. Having
solid, proven systems will get you through!

SEPTEMBER 18

Before you dive into a task or project, ask yourself, "WHY am I doing it? What is the goal?"

■   ■   ■

Use the answers you come up with as the driving force behind your actions. Keep your eye on the purpose and goal.

SEPTEMBER 19

*Get in the habit of looking over an
email before you hit SEND.*

■ ■ ■

Have you stated your purpose clearly? If there is
action required, list a response date. Check for
spelling, grammar and if you meant to attach a
document or file, be sure that you actually did!

SEPTEMBER 20

Find places to work that
inspire creativity.

▨   ▨   ▨

If you need time to be innovative and creative
today, find a place where you can work as
interruption-free as possible for an extended
period of time. In order to achieve flow, you need
to find or create an environment for yourself
where you are not switching tasks frequently or
getting interrupted.

SEPTEMBER 21

Lesson Learned:

▨　▨　▨

Keeping the hours of someone who tended to be a workaholic was causing major issues for a man whose wife finally read him the riot act. He needed to find more time in his life for his wife and children or she wanted a divorce. He began setting an alarm on his phone an hour prior to when he needed to leave the office. It alerted him to finish up his work, make his plan for the following day, and leave on time. He's home for dinner most nights and still happily married.

SEPTEMBER 22

*Put away files and materials
before moving on to the next
activity or project.*

■ ■ ■

Develop the habit of keeping your workspace
clear to work on one project at a time. It will
alleviate piles and stacks and will also help keep
your mind clear.

SEPTEMBER 23

Make good use of your down time.

■　■　■

Create a "rainy day list" of things to do. If you are fortunate to have occasions when things slow down, take advantage of the opportunity to get caught up. Having a list of tasks and projects you want to get done will keep you from wasting precious time trying to figure out how to make the best of the slow time.

SEPTEMBER 24

*Batch and then process
your tasks today.*

▦　▦　▦

If you find yourself overwhelmed with the items
that come at you today, remember to batch them
into categories (paper, email, voicemail, thoughts
and requests) and process each of them the same
way: toss or delete, delegate, do it now, file for
reference or take action later. Use this process
for dealing with all categories of information in
the exact same manner.

SEPTEMBER 25

*Be sure to take some
YOU time today!*

■　■　■

Get some exercise. Escape to the local coffee
shop with a magazine. Take a nap. Go shopping.
Whether it's 10 minutes or an hour, taking time
for yourself will give you the energy you need to
be productive.

SEPTEMBER 26

Strive to be on time.

■   ■   ■

Arrive on time for your appointments whether they are business or personal. Set a timer or alarm if you need to and make sure you account for travel time (even if it's just down the hall) so you are not late to meetings or appointments. Being on time is not only professional but it also shows respect for others. If you are running late, try to send word by phone or message when you will arrive.

SEPTEMBER 27

Keep the information you email to people at work professional.

■　■　■

Avoid the temptation to send jokes, stories and chain emails at work. Your colleagues have enough email to deal with without receiving this type of spam.

▧　▧　▧

The shorter way to do many things

is to do only one thing at a time.

— Mozart

SEPTEMBER 29

Communicate consistently and effectively when working as a team.

■   ■   ■

If you are involved in a project or activity that requires high volumes of communication between multiple people, consider scheduling regular meetings, conference calls or web conferencing to minimize unproductive email conversations. Email is not always the most effective mode of communication. Thanks to today's technology, there are other highly effective options available, especially when people involved are in multiple locations.

SEPTEMBER 30

Develop a system for storing articles you want to save.

▓   ▓   ▓

Cut down on the paper you need to organize by saving reference materials in digital form. Scan articles from magazines or journals you want to keep and then pass on or recycle the publication so it's not taking up space in your work area. Develop a good digital filing system for them.

OCTOBER 1

*Stay offline when you
are on the phone.*

▨ ▨ ▨

When you are talking on the telephone, eliminate the temptation to read email or surf the
web. Minimize your email, turn off your monitor
or turn your back on your computer. Giving
someone your complete focus is important and
shows respect.

OCTOBER 2

Schedule a date with yourself to do a quarterly review of your goals.

▦ ▦ ▦

Do a progress check and update your goals accordingly. To achieve success, goals need to be assessed and re-assessed. And what a great opportunity to see the progress you've made!

OCTOBER 3

Keep your contact list current.

■　■　■

When you meet someone new either in person or via email, be disciplined about putting their contact information into your contacts. You'll thank yourself the next time you want to call or email them.

OCTOBER 4

Is your in-basket in the best location?

■   ■   ■

Your in-basket should be in a place that is convenient for people to leave things but not in your central work zone so it's disrupting to you. Wall pockets just outside your workspace are effective, or a box in the mailroom if it's close.

OCTOBER 5

Lesson Learned:

■   ■   ■

Putting her cell phone in her top drawer increased an employee's focus. Seeing it on her desk was a distraction every time a text or voice-mail arrived. She checked it occasionally and got more work done than ever.

OCTOBER 6

*File meeting notes and
materials right away.*

■   ■   ■

After attending a meeting, take a few minutes to
put away any resources or files you used before
moving on to your next task. File the folders
where they belong so you can keep a productive
work space throughout your day and you won't
have a huge mess to deal with at the end of
the day.

OCTOBER 7

Take 5 minutes to do NOTHING today!

▧   ▧   ▧

Sometimes the best thing to do with your time is to do NOTHING. Doing NOTHING is healthy for your body, mind and soul. It is reinvigorating and refreshing, whether you choose to sit back and close your eyes, go outside and watch the clouds, or sit and people-watch... Enjoy!

OCTOBER 8

Schedule time on your calendar
for catching up after a trip.

■ ■ ■

When you schedule out of office time for a business trip, make an effort to schedule a block of time when you return to the office for "re-entry." You'll need time to catch up as well as to take action on tasks that arose during your travels. Knowing you have the time blocked will make for a less stressful and more productive return from your trip.

OCTOBER 9

Find a way to help someone today.

■   ■   ■

Whether it's helping on a project at work, or at the grocery store, or signing up to volunteer at an event or organization, making a difference in the lives of others will improve your self-worth. Helping others helps you live a richer life.

OCTOBER 10

Practice good tech etiquette.

■   ■   ■

If you need to respond to a phone call or text during a meeting or social event, have the courtesy to excuse yourself. It's the polite thing to do!

OCTOBER 11

*Schedule regular appointments
with yourself to file paperwork.*

■   ■   ■

Filing isn't typically an activity that people love
to do—it may even be right up there with getting
a root canal, but it's a necessity. Done on a
routine basis (daily or weekly), it will stay under
control. Consider starting your own "no pile
Fridays" so you can leave work knowing you'll
come back to a clean workspace on Monday.

■ ■ ■

Every great dream begins with a dreamer. Always remember, you have within you the strength, the patience, and the passion to reach for the stars to change the world.

— *Harriet Tubman*

OCTOBER 13

*Batch tasks to improve
your productivity.*

■ ■ ■

Review what you need to do today and batch like
tasks together as much as possible. To make the
most of your time, block time when you'll make
your phone calls. Have another block of time for
writing email, another block of time for running
errands. Batching tasks is a much more efficient
use of your time.

OCTOBER 14

Share your passion with others.

■ ■ ■

Volunteer at an organization where you can do what you are passionate about. Making a commitment to share your passion is a great way to make sure other parts of your life don't get in the way of doing what you love.

OCTOBER 15

Are you procrastinating because you need help? Just ask.

■   ■   ■

Is there something on your to-do list that you've been putting off because you need help? Maybe you didn't realize you need help at first, or maybe you didn't know who to ask, or maybe you just didn't get around to asking. Whichever it is, make the call, get the assistance you need and get it done. It feels so good!

OCTOBER 16

Schedule time(s) to process
your email on a daily basis.

▨ ▨ ▨

Email can distract you for hours if you let it.
Process it in batches just as you process your
paper mail. Schedule several times of day and
even use a timer if you are concerned about
losing track of time.

OCTOBER 17

*Be mindful of the pace
of your life today.*

■　■　■

Are you happy with the speed your day is
moving? Do you need to add some tasks or
activities if it's not full enough? Or do you need
to eliminate some if there's too much going on
and your head is whirling? Taking a moment
to reflect can help you make necessary
adjustments.

Work toward excellence,
not perfection.

■ ■ ■

If you tend to be a perfectionist and things are never good enough, make an effort to change your mindset to working toward excellence and enjoying the journey. Being a perfectionist can be tense and stressful, whereas participating in mastering a task brings joy and happiness. Lighten up and have fun!

OCTOBER 19

Lesson Learned:

■ ■ ■

After learning how to create systems to manage his email and paper, a manager let out a huge sigh and was thrilled to be back in control. He realized he'd been letting his inbox, paper and stacks of stuff control him.

OCTOBER 20

Take steps to eliminate junk mail.

■　■　■

Do you get too much junk mail or too many catalogs? There are several organizations you can contact to eliminate it. Google "how to eliminate junk mail or catalogs" for current resources. Save time and frustration as well as a few trees!

*Build travel time into your
schedule.*

■   ■   ■

When you are planning your schedule, actually
enter your travel time as a calendar event so that
you plan ample time, not only for the appointment, but to get there AND return! (If your job
consists of regular travel to off-site locations,
consider starting a spreadsheet to track travel
times to frequent locations so you always have
the information at hand.)

OCTOBER 22

Plan for breaks away from work.

■   ■   ■

Do your best to have a vacation or a "stay-cation" on the calendar whether it's a short-term or long-term plan. Plan some activities you enjoy so you have something to look forward to. Taking time out is refreshing and will refuel you to be more productive upon your return.

OCTOBER 23

Take time to purge the stuff that's accumulated in your office.

■ ■ ■

How many pens, post-it pads and coffee cups do you really need? Many supplies in your work-space have a way of multiplying and chances are you don't even notice. Take a few minutes to sort through your supplies today and keep only what you need.

OCTOBER 24

Address one subject per email.

■　　■　　■

If you have multiple issues to cover in an email, it may be most effective to send separate emails or be sure to let your recipient know you have several different topics you are covering in one email. Either of these approaches will provide a better likelihood of all your issues being addressed. If multiple topics are covered in one email, use bullet points or numbers to ensure they are noted as separate items.

Do your best to keep work at work.

■   ■   ■

70% of Americans work evenings or weekends, the majority doing so because of "self-imposed pressure." Be sure you are aware of your organization's expectations for you to work outside the office. You might be surprised at the things that can wait and don't need to be brought home to finish.

OCTOBER 26

■ ■ ■

The greatest power a person

possesses is the power to choose.

— *J. Martin Kohe*

OCTOBER 27

Make good choices throughout your day to maximize your energy.

■   ■   ■

Your choices will either energize you or zap you. If you are struggling with low energy levels, evaluate the choices you are making about your diet, exercise and sleep patterns to see if you can make different choices to increase your energy.

OCTOBER 28

Avoid task switching for optimal productivity.

■   ■   ■

If you want to work more slowly, intentionally and in a more relaxed fashion, minimize interruptions as well as switching back and forth between tasks. Task switching results in a higher level of stress, frustration, mental effort, and an increased sense of time pressure. That's a high cost to pay!

OCTOBER 29

As you plan your day today,
schedule more time for tasks
than you think it will take.

■　■　■

A rule of thumb is to plan one and half times the
amount of time you think you need to complete a
task. It is better to have time left over in your
schedule than to come up short.

OCTOBER 30

Turn off the notifiers on your inbox (the auditory 'ding' and the ghost window).

■   ■   ■

Email notifiers are a huge distraction. Without them you'll be much more focused! You'll be amazed at how much work you'll get done!

OCTOBER 31

Update your calendar regularly.

■   ■   ■

Choose one day a week to make sure your calendar is up to date with events, appointments and meetings. If you have a spouse or partner or children at home, consider a once-a-week "calendar check-in" where you update the family calendar with items to ensure you all know where you need to be. (If you use Outlook® or Google Calendar, consider sharing calendars to simplify this process.)

NOVEMBER 3

Create zones for like items.
Put them in well-labeled containers.

▨　▨　▨

It's so easy for things like car chargers, technology cables, sunglasses, and office supplies to get strewn around. Designate specific locations for these items, find a container that is suitable and label it so it's easy to read. Save time in your day by having a place to put those things where you can find them when you need them!

NOVEMBER 4

Just do it – and do it now!

■　■　■

If you have short tasks you can do quickly (in a minute or two), just get them done! In many instances, by the time you write yourself a note or figure out where to put something so you can find it again to do later, you could have done the deed.

NOVEMBER 5

Begin to prepare for the holiday rush.

■   ■   ■

The holidays are just around the corner. Consider putting your holiday events on the calendar now so you can be ahead of the game with your plan-ning. Scheduling events either before or after the rush has its benefits! The holidays are a time to enjoy. The less last minute planning you have to do, the more joyful they will be.

*Surround yourself
with positive people.*

▪   ▪   ▪

Take a look at the people in your life. Are they
lifting you up or dragging you down? Make
choices to invest in relationships with positive
people. You are much happier and more productive when you have people in your life who
are energy boosters, not energy suckers!

NOVEMBER 7

Block a transition day
before your vacation.

■　■　■

On your calendar, block off the day before you leave on vacation so you won't schedule meetings or clients. Having time to prepare for being gone makes all the difference in the world in being ready to go!

NOVEMBER 8

*Create a strategy for dealing
with the "unexpecteds."*

▩   ▩   ▩

Unexpecteds can almost be guaranteed on a
daily basis. They are a part of life, whether it's a
flat tire, an appointment cancelling, or technology crashing. Anticipating how you will
handle them makes all the difference in the
world. Breathing deeply is critical. Taking a brief
time-out in order to respond mindfully and with
a good plan of action will be much more effective
than letting emotions take over and reacting.

■　■　■

What the world really needs
is more love and less paperwork.

— *Pearl Bailey*

Start fresh with your inbox.

■   ■   ■

If you are tired of an overloaded inbox and want a fresh start with "inbox zero" or at least not having to scroll, create a folder where you can move all the email in your inbox. Begin today processing every email that comes in by either **deleting, forwarding, replying, saving, or putting it in your action system**. You'll feel SO good to take control of your inbox. Disciplining yourself to make one of these five decisions listed is critical so it doesn't fill up again!

NOVEMBER 11

Organize a service project or a volunteer opportunity for you and your team during the holidays.

■　　■　　■

There's no better gift than helping others. Consider working with local food banks, schools, churches, charitable organizations or civic groups. Service projects can be excellent opportunities for team building.

Take time to reprioritize when you take on something new.

◼   ◼   ◼

You are constantly finishing tasks and projects as well as taking on new things. When you add something new to your to-do list, take the time to shuffle what's there to keep your priorities and deadlines in check.

NOVEMBER 13

*When you get overwhelmed,
instead of going harder, STOP!*

■   ■   ■

It's counterintuitive, but by doing so, your
productivity will improve. Take time to adjust
the choices you have made: be more realistic
with your time; say NO to requests that aren't
consistent with your goals; re-prioritize so you
are focusing on important vs. urgent items; stop
procrastinating, etc. Shift your thinking and you
will see positive results.

Create file folders or a digital list for the various regular meetings you attend.

■   ■   ■

Put notes, ideas and reminders here of things you want to discuss at the next session. Having an organized system eliminates the stress of trying to remember these thoughts.

NOVEMBER 15

*Get the most out of
your reading time.*

▓ ▓ ▓

Before you begin reading an article, book or
newsletter, do a "brain dump" of anything on
your mind that will keep you from being focused
on what you are about to read. Get your mind
into the zone of what you are reading and why
you are reading it.

NOVEMBER 16

Lesson Learned:

■   ■   ■

When the topic of the email "ghost window" being a major distractor was discussed, a staff member said that he absolutely could NOT turn it off and that seeing that preview was critical to his being on top of his work. Finally agreeing to turn it off for a one week trial, he reported on day two, "I can't believe how much I am getting done!"

NOVEMBER 17

*Begin thinking of creative
ideas for holiday gifts.*

※　　※　　※

As the holidays approach, you may be starting to
rack your brain for gift ideas. Consider giving
"consumable" gifts (things that people can eat or
drink). Also consider the idea of giving an
experience—potentially one that you can do
together. Have a SIMPLIFY theme for the
holidays — holidays don't have to be full of
STUFF!

NOVEMBER 18

Tackle a project you are avoiding.

■   ■   ■

What do you need to get done today that you just are NOT looking forward to doing? Get it done PRONTO! It's so easy to put off things that you don't want to do. Getting them done first feels good and makes the rest of the day a piece of cake.

NOVEMBER 19

If you plan to declutter your space, consider asking someone to help you and act as a "throw-away partner."

■   ■   ■

You will most likely let go of more unnecessary things if you have someone asking good questions and coaching you along. You'll develop good momentum as you work together.

When you attend a meeting or presentation, only take the technology you absolutely need.

■   ■   ■

Don't be a distraction to yourself and those nearby. If you must take items with on/off buttons, power them down. Go electronics free if you can.

*Try to keep your day
evenly paced today.*

■　■　■

Do some rescheduling if there are an unrealistic
number of things on your calendar. Only so
much can be done in a day. Be realistic about
what you can truly accomplish. Reschedule or
opt out of activities and non-critical meetings if
your calendar is overbooked.

As you work on a project, anticipate there will be roadblocks.

■　■　■

It's inevitable. Learn to be flexible and adjust your project plan accordingly. Build extra time into your project deadlines for the "unexpecteds" in order to minimize the stress of roadblocks.

■ ■ ■

What you get by achieving your goals is not as important as what you **become** *by achieving your goals. — Henry David Thoreau*

Plan your day so you can get adequate sleep.

■ ■ ■

Research shows that 95% of humans require 7-8 hours per night. Studies show that without enough sleep people are less productive and more cranky. Avoid sabotaging your own efforts to be productive by staying up too late.

Schedule a date on your calendar to set annual personal and professional goals.

■   ■   ■

Clear goals will help you make wise decisions about how to spend your time. It's like having a roadmap—without goals, you may find yourself wandering places you don't want to go.

NOVEMBER 26

Consider reducing your paper by scanning documents and storing them digitally.

■   ■   ■

There are fast, simple scanners available that can help you have less paper to pile and file. Developing a solid organization system for your digital files is critical for this to be the answer to being organized.

*Take in and appreciate
today's every moment!*

▩   ▩   ▩

You may be familiar with Bill Keane's quote: "Yesterday's the **past**, **tomorrow's** the **future**, but **today** is a gift. That's why it's called the present." Planning ahead is a necessity but too much can take away from being in the present. Learn from the past but don't camp out there. Be in the NOW!

NOVEMBER 28

Think twice when addressing email to a group of people.

▦   ▦   ▦

Put a recipient's email addresses in the bcc: line if they don't need to reply to the entire group. When they click "Reply to All" their response will only be sent to you. You can help alleviate the rampant "Reply to All" phenomenon. The others in the group will thank you!

Keep your letters, reports and emails brief whenever possible.

▦ ▦ ▦

Remember every word you write, someone must read! Consider using bullet points to break up large amounts of text and be sure that action items and due dates are clear. Adopt a "less is more" mindset.

NOVEMBER 30

Lesson Learned:

■　■　■

An employee found herself checking email every 4-5 minutes and was unable to get her work done because of the constant email interruption. She thought checking that frequently was expected of her in the event there was an urgent matter. A conversation with her manager revealed she was only expected her to check email 2-3 times each day. The manager reminded her that if there was an emergency, she would receive a phone call or a knock at the door. Suddenly, she was able to get her work done!

DECEMBER 1

Plan ahead for holiday events.

■   ■   ■

Add holiday events to your calendar when you receive the invitation. Purchase any gifts necessary in advance. Planning ahead this time of year will help minimize stress and keep you in the holiday spirit!

DECEMBER 2

As you launch your day today, think about the things and people you are passionate about outside of work.

■   ■   ■

Keep these passions in mind in order to motivate you to be as effective and productive as possible during your day so you'll have time and energy for the things that truly matter. It's a great step in working toward "life-work balance!"

DECEMBER 3

Keep meetings on track.

■   ■   ■

When you are at a meeting, either large or small, use the "parking lot" technique to record off-topic comments or questions by writing them on a flip chart or white board and return to them later. It's easy to head down a rabbit trail at meetings when odd topics come up. Having a strategy to deal with unrelated issues will help keep your meeting on track.

DECEMBER 4

*Be conscious about acquiring
new stuff for your office.*

▓ ▓ ▓

Before you purchase something new, be certain
you have the need (and place) for it. Buy only
what you'll truly use otherwise it becomes "stuff"
that you'll be purging at a later date!

DECEMBER 5

Pick one or two email folders
to purge today.

▨　▨　▨

Clean out old emails. Do this every day for a
week or two and you'll get up to date. Email
folders don't get purged as often as they should.
It doesn't take long to do and the payoff is great.

DECEMBER 6

Think twice about how you choose to communicate.

■   ■   ■

When you need to choose a mode of communication to connect with people today, take a minute to determine what's best: a text, email, face-to-face visit, instant message, phone call, etc. Consider the preferences of each recipient and the timeliness of your information or any response required.

■　■　■

Always bear in mind that your own resolution to succeed is more important than any other.

— Abraham Lincoln

DECEMBER 8

Review the vacation schedule for your team or organization as soon as it's available.

■ ■ ■

The sooner you know when there may be extra demands on you the better, so you can plan accordingly. As holiday vacations are announced, look for conflicts with potential deadlines or areas that may need extra coverage when people on your team might be out of the office.

DECEMBER 9

Schedule time on your calendar to process information after attending meetings.

■ ■ ■

In order to process action items following a meeting, schedule 15 minutes on your calendar before you dive into the next thing. This allows you to create any action items resulting from a meeting as well as to give you the time to organize related paperwork instead of leaving it in a pile on your desk.

DECEMBER 10

Check in with your vendors or suppliers for their holiday schedules.

■　■　■

It's helpful to know in advance so you can adjust deadlines to cover for holiday closures and/or shipping issues. Do what it takes to keep your clients and customers happy!

DECEMBER 11

*Know what your priorities
are today.*

▓   ▓   ▓

With all the things there are to get accomplished
in a day, it can be easy to dive into the low-value
tasks first. Be sure you know what is most
important and work to get those items checked
off your list at the beginning of the day.

DECEMBER 12

*Leave an out of office message
when you are on vacation.*

■　■　■

Remember to leave a message on your voicemail
as well as an auto-responder on your email,
letting people know you are out of the office and
when you'll return. Let them know you are
unavailable until then. Enjoy your time away
without feeling as though you need to respond to
messages. If people have that expectation, you
don't have to worry about follow up until you
return to the office.

DECEMBER 13

Carve out creative time in your day.

■ ■ ■

Allow for creative time during your day whether it's during your commute to and from work, taking a walk, during your workout, in conversation with colleagues or friends, or just during quiet time. Keep a journal or a tape recorder to collect your ideas, dreams and thoughts. Sometimes the day can slip by with too much structure. Creative time for your brain is valuable.

DECEMBER 14

Lesson Learned:

▓   ▓   ▓

A very busy business owner had been extremely scattered and unable to keep any organization to her action items and things were regularly falling through the cracks. She began carrying Capture Cards with her and writing down everything! She reports, "They saved my life!"

DECEMBER 15

*Plan ahead for your
holiday vacation.*

■　■　■

If you are planning time away from the office
during the holidays, make sure co-workers have
what they need to cover for you and to follow up
on projects while you are gone. With good planning and communication, you'll be able to
minimize any hiccups so you can relax during
your vacation, knowing that things at the office
are in good hands.

DECEMBER 16

Sort your incoming mail immediately.

▦　▦　▦

Recycle junk mail, shred documents with sensitive or personal information, designate specific locations to put your reading material and information that needs to be filed, and place any action items in your in-basket or action file. Having a system for processing mail allows you to take care of it immediately instead of letting it pile up.

DECEMBER 17

*Handle frequent interruptions
professionally.*

▨　▨　▨

Be aware of "frequent offenders" of interruptions. If you find this is an issue with
someone, ask them to keep a list of questions or
tasks and arrange a regular time to get together
to deal with them at once. It's most productive
for both of you!

DECEMBER 18

Set boundaries for checking in while away from the office.

■　■　■

If checking email or phone messages over the holidays is critical, set clear boundaries and time frames to do it. Allow yourself time to stay connected, but remember your vacation is your time to refuel!

DECEMBER 19

If you have email folders or digital file folders that you use frequently, locate them at the top of the list.

■ ■ ■

Place a number or punctuation symbol at the beginning of the file name. It's handy to not have to scroll through alphabetized folders to find the ones you utilize most.

*Visualize your progress
on challenging projects.*

■   ■   ■

When you are faced with a challenging task or project today, take a moment to close your eyes, relax and visualize how the task or project will pan out. "See" it through from beginning to end, including the dynamite feeling you'll have once it's completed. Visualization is a powerful tool that will increase your confidence and help you achieve success.

■ ■ ■

Often, he who does too much,

does too little.

— *Italian Proverb*

DECEMBER 22

*Count your successes before
you leave work each day.*

■　　■　　■

It's easy to finish up the day bemoaning the
things that didn't get done. Before you leave the
office or before you turn off the light tonight,
take time to think of all you accomplished in
your day. Be sure to take time to reflect on all
that you DID do. Give yourself a high five!

DECEMBER 23

*Use slower seasons to
catch up on projects.*

※ ※ ※

If the holiday season is a slow time of year for
you at the office, take advantage of the opportunity to catch up on tasks or projects that have
been put on the back burner. Consider this time
a gift! (If it's a busy time of year, keep a list or file
of the tasks you'll need to address after the
holidays.)

DECEMBER 24

*Practice listening
without interrupting.*

■   ■   ■

When you are with people today, either in meetings or at home having conversations with your
family, give them your full attention. It feels good
to be an attentive listener. People realize you
care. This will energize both them and you.
When you feel good, good things happen.

DECEMBER 25

Make your "people time"
high quality. Be in the moment
with them.

▨   ▨   ▨

Having quality relationships is very important
and often gets compromised with the ever
presence of technology. Don't let it interfere with
your relationships.

DECEMBER 26

*Use a timer to help
monitor your time.*

■ ■ ■

A timer is a useful tool to ensure that you don't
go overtime. If you want to spend 30 minutes
working on a project, or 20 minutes processing
email, set your timer and you can dive into your
work without worrying about the time. The
buzzer will let you know when it's time to wrap
up and move on.

DECEMBER 27

Find ways to spend less time sitting.

■   ■   ■

Sitting at a desk for an extended period of time isn't good for your health. Find reasons to stand up by doing things such as standing up to take phone calls, walking the stairs on your break, or setting a timer as a cue to get up and stretch. Research studies show that a few minutes of activity throughout the day can offset the negative effects of long-term sitting.

DECEMBER 28

Lesson Learned:

■   ■   ■

A manager and her team became total believers in the Capture Card concept. It changed their worlds, individually and as a team. Staff could frequently be seen walking down the halls exchanging Capture Cards with to-do items for each other!

DECEMBER 29

Review the organization of your digital documents.

■　■　■

Look at the structure you use to organize both your email folders and document files. It can be helpful to create a file map that you use in both locations. Take time to reorganize if it's necessary. Consistency will help you when you file information as well as when you need to retrieve it.

DECEMBER 30

What is a new habit you are
trying to instill today?

■   ■   ■

With a felt tip marker put a black dot on your
thumb or palm, or write the new habit you want
to start on a card and place it in a visible
location. Frequent notice of these simple,
practical reminders will help you make the
positive changes you want to implement!

DECEMBER 31

Find a quiet spot to reflect on your growth and newly improved habits!

■ ■ ■

Celebrate a SIMPLER life as you look to begin a new year. In what ways is your life more peaceful and more productive with your new work and life habits? Congratulate yourself on the progress you've made and start contemplating new goals for the coming year.

FINAL THOUGHTS

Share your stories...

I hope you've been encouraged by this book! Productivity isn't necessarily a destination but a journey. I would welcome hearing your stories of success and how making *SIMPLIFY! One Day at a Time* a part of your daily life has helped you on your journey. Drop me a note at:

P.O. Box 443, Camp Sherman, OR, 97730

or bethanne@simplifynw.com.

Tap into Bethanne as a resource for your organization...

I'm passionate about helping others make progress in their efforts to find improved focus, productivity and life/work balance. If I can be a resource to you or your organization in your efforts in these areas, please contact me at bethanne@simplifynw.com to find out more about workshops, presentations, keynotes and individual coaching opportunities. Visit www.simplifynw.com to learn more about SIMPLIFY!.

Sharing the gift of productivity...

If you have enjoyed ***SIMPLIFY! One Day at a Time*** and want to share the valuable resources with others in your organization or network, contact us to find out about quantity discounts (info@simplifynw.com).

Special thanks...

Thanks to my friends, family, clients and colleagues who have encouraged me to write this book.

Special thanks to Dave and Kim. Dave, you have been incredibly patient as this project has consumed much of my time, and ours, too! You have given me such valuable support and feedback. Thank you.

Kim, your tireless support and encouragement are most appreciated. You've provided tremendous wisdom and knowledge. I couldn't have done this project without both of you!

SIMPLIFY!

■   ■   ■

Live Simply. Simply Live.

www.simplifynw.com

Made in the USA
Charleston, SC
30 November 2014